FOREVER

The Art
of Lifetime
Relationships

J A N E T   B L Y

Aglow Publications

A Ministry of Women's Aglow Fellowship, Int'l.
P.O. Box 1548
Lynnwood, WA 98046-1558
USA

Cover design by Ray Braun

Unless otherwise noted, all scripture quotations in this publication are from the Holy Bible, New International Version. Copyright 1973, 1978, 1984, International Bible Society.

ISBN 0-932305-84-9

DEDICATION

To Steve . . .
who's already given me
a lifetime's worth of love

Contents

CONTENTS

Introduction

A mother. A father. Sisters and brothers. A favorite aunt. A surviving grandparent. And later, my husband. I had saved my lifetime obligations for a precious few.

Other relationships were optional. Either they happened, or they didn't.

Then I entered the association of followers of Jesus. An explosive variety of new family members confronted my priority list. Jesus had strong words about their importance.

"All men will know that you are my disciples if you love one another" (John 13:35).

Those with whom I will spend eternity don't have to give me the time of day. We all have our crippling personality defects, as well as rich background resources and boundaries of experience in, and motivation for, enduring relationships.

Friendship with God doesn't automatically produce the ability to get along with people. But wanting to is one big step forward.

In the world, risking relationships means fullness of life as God intended it. His grace to a lonely, fallen creation.

In the church, it means spiritual power. Allowing another person close enough to generate a spurt of growth, a flash of insight. Knowing and caring enough about others to pray without ceasing. Preparing ourselves in the nitty-gritty of earth's trials for the glories ahead with our eternal Father, the heavenly hosts, and the great cloud of witnesses.

This book grows out of years of observation and study as I've grappled with the pain and dishonor of the enigma of love turned sour. Crumbled marriages. Deserted children. Embittered friendships. Broken partnerships.

I also realize that, no matter how hard we try, some of these sorrows will always be with us. That's the nature of the earthly system. Out of kilter. Rebellious. Insensitive. This side of heaven.

Even so, much of the brokenness is preventable. Many relationships deteriorate because of neglect and ignorance. Because no one took the time or trouble necessary to attempt to practice the principles of the art, the very learnable art, of cultivating lifetime relationships.

Janet Chester Bly
June 6, 1990
Winchester, Idaho

1
...
Why Love
a Lifetime?

Lifetime relationships don't just happen.

Someone has to make a conscious effort to care and to persevere, or relationships stagnate and die.

Someone has to build bridges.

Someone has to work through the warts, tangles, and land mines of people problems.

Someone has to provide the time and space needed for a comfy corner of companionship where give-and-take, trial-and-error, forgive-and-forbear can be rehearsed.

How many of us remember being taught the fine art of making and keeping relationships? Who has ever impressed upon us the reasons why we should even try? No, what we learned in kindergarten isn't enough.

Maggie Karenns is one of those rare people who values a multitude of lifetime relationships. She works at it. Full-time.

MAGGIE

Every morning, Maggie sweeps her hair into a stylish pearl comb, struggles into her leg braces, and pulls herself by crutches into the dining room. She plops down into a comfortable, cushioned chair and spreads out a large yearly appointment book. Each day on every month has at least one name scrawled on it. Soon, Maggie's India ink pen will sweep back and forth over cream-colored stationery; perhaps she'll search through a pile of greeting cards looking for acknowledgement of a birthday, an anniversary, or a congratulation of some sort.

Maggie has a lot of time on her hands.

Being crippled by polio at age twenty didn't stop her from pursuing a job as a medical technician or teaching fourth graders at Calvary Presbyterian Church for twenty-five years. Now she's a widow and retired. She still feels a lump of sadness when she thinks of the two sons she had for such a short time. Neither lived longer than two years.

But Maggie's not the kind to indulge in self-pity. When she could no longer work or teach and had no family to tend, she began to search for purpose by reaching out in the only way she knew. From her home. To people she already knew.

She began by writing cards, notes, and letters to a few of her former students. When she received several enthusiastic responses, she was encouraged to keep on. Now, she's corresponded with every one of the hundreds of students she ever had, while keeping up with a swarm of relatives and friends. Many write back or come by to visit regularly.

Like Suzanne. And Dave.

Suzanne

Suzanne Viegas now lives in the neighboring county

with her three pre-schoolers and truck-driver husband. Every time she passes Venice City on her way to the doctor, she thinks of Maggie. Today she'll stop by, three kids in tow, because she knows that, though it's been twenty years since she attended Mrs. Karenns's class, she'll be warmly remembered and welcomed.

Suzanne's family moved three states away shortly after she attended Mrs. Karenns's class. Through her parents' divorce, a succession of babysitters, many more moves, and rocky teenage traumas, Maggie's steady caring was the only stable relationship Suzanne knew. Maggie wrote to her at least once a year and even called when she graduated from high school.

Today, she'll pour out some of her grown-up struggles. "I never had a girlfriend longer than one year at a time. None of my school teachers tried to single out a skinny, shy loner. My older brother and sister have always lived with my father and stepmother. Boyfriends came and went in my mother's life. The only thing I knew about my relatives I learned one afternoon at a family reunion when I was eleven. Now, I'm supposed to know how to relate to a husband, a man who often seems like a stranger to me?"

With a Bible close by and a wealth of wisdom and experiences, Maggie listens and advises.

Maggie's a faithful friend and counselor. She has even been a lifesaver.

Dave

"Your note arrived today," a young man in his early thirties wrote. "I had full intentions of ending it all by blowing my brains out. It's that bad. Struggling to accept myself after the amputation gets me down. I still haven't gotten over Brenda [his former girlfriend]. You made me recall all you've had to go through, the happier days of my childhood, and God. Perhaps there's still hope. Please pray for me. Love, Dave. P.S. Please don't worry. I locked the gun in my brother's cabinet."

Life would be so much poorer for Suzanne and Dave if they didn't have this lifetime friend. In return, they provide Maggie a reason to keep going each day.

Everyone needs a "Maggie Karenns." We need someone to care for us through all the ups and downs and ins and outs of changes and disappointments. We also need her kind of example to encourage us in what Bill Moyers, the television journalist, calls "a love of sharing, a passion for connecting."[1]

Friends Forever explores the why and how of increasing our ability to care and connect with people who have entered our sphere of acquaintance by chance and choice.

The world is crammed with humans. None of us should have any trouble knowing as many of them as we want. That is, in superficial ways. By name and occupation. By an address. By what they think of the weather.

Or in occasional ways. When they happen to parallel our side of the freeway or wait in the same line.

We might strive for longer term interactions: Until they move to Georgia. After they've pulled us out of a funk we're in. Or when they stop sending Christmas cards.

Isn't that enough?

Why should we pursue the awesome goal of making friends for life?

WHY LIFETIME RELATIONSHIPS?

Lifetime Relationships Were Established for Our Good

"The Lord God said, 'It is not good for the man to be alone. I will make a helper suitable for him' " (Gen. 2:18).

God created the ties of lifetime liaisons, bound by commitment, pledged by blood and genes.

A man cherishes a wife.

A mother sides with her child.

A daughter nurses an aging parent.

A grandfather leaves a rich heritage.

The family would spawn temples and city halls and national flags. A man and woman would have personal reasons to live and, if need be, to die to preserve good and fight evil. The well-being of people they loved, people with their name and history and progeny, depended on it.

When that basic familial bond is broken . . .

> individuals wither
> > communities falter
> > > nations fail.

Something sacred and essential dies. Generations stumble until lifetime links are redeemed again.

Clyde M. Narramore said, "The establishing of a great family is the most important, far-reaching accomplishment in the world. It is far greater than designing the Golden Gate or Verrazano Narrows bridges, far greater than composing 'Silent Night' or painting 'The Last Supper.' A great family is 'big business.' "[2]

Jonathan Edwards, a great preacher and theologian in the 1700's, was never called "Mr. Personality." Sickly, nearly blind, a genius, and a zealous perfectionist, his chief fault was his inability to work well at close quarters with others. However, he had the insight and fortune to marry an understanding wife.

Sarah Pierpont Edwards maintained a "genial and attractive hospitality until her home became like a sanctuary to multitudes."[3] She also succeeded at loving relationships with Jonathan, their eight daughters, three sons, and seventy-five grandchildren.

He, too, learned to value relationships. Reverend Edwards "deeply influenced many people . . . through his correspondence and writing. . . . Through personal contact, he left his mark upon great men and common people."[4]

Even more notable is the history of their descendants. Of the more than four hundred who have been traced, fourteen became college presidents; one hundred were or are college professors; and one hundred have been ministers, missionaries, or theologians. More than one hundred were lawyers and judges, sixty were doctors, and as many more became authors or editors. It has been estimated than every major industry in America has been touched by one or more of the Edwards clan.[5]

Lifetime Relationships Help Us Emotionally

Author Dee Brestin claims, "I cannot count the number of times I have been strengthened by another woman's heart-felt hug, appreciative note, surprise gift, or caring question. If my best friends were simply buddies, I doubt I'd work hard at keeping them. But my women friends are an oasis to me, encouraging me to go on. They are essential to my well-being."[6]

Beyond the family, lifetime friends are crucial. Most relatives are ours by forces beyond our control. Friends are the relationships we choose.

In our fast-paced, frantic, mobile society, it's easy to neglect relationships. Yet the shifting, uncertain, even fearful mood of our times requires that we relate to people who will keep us accountable, provide a network of comfort and safety, and remind us that we matter, that our lives mean something to them.

My husband and I have moved to more than twenty different locations while we've been married. In almost every instance, I've managed to maintain at least one permanent friendship in each town. Except that year we lived in Sacramento.

My husband was an administrative assistant to a California state assemblyman, so he worked at the state capitol. I was tied to the needs of our year-old infant son, and I never felt comfortable initiating contacts with our neighbors in that one-hundred unit, four-story complex. I call that my "lost year." I felt so lonely and insignificant. No faces, no shared laughter or tears, no people adventures are associated with that period. We just existed. I still think of Sacramento as an impersonal megalopolis, not a place to call home. Hardly even a former residence. People could have made a difference.

Children need faithful friends, too. Even if their own families are falling apart, another adult can insulate them from turmoil and pain. Research scientists are creating a composite of what causes children to become resilient or vulnerable.

A study of nearly seven hundred children born in 1955 on the Hawaiian island of Kauai to impoverished families, with one or both parents either alcoholic or mentally ill and with the added problem of trauma at birth, such as oxygen deprivation or forceps delivery, showed one child in ten could withstand the difficulties. In fact, that one developed exceptionally well.

"Without exception, all the children who thrived had at least one person that provided them consistent emotional support—a grandmother, an older sister, a teacher or a neighbor," said Emmy Warner, a psychologist at the University of California at Davis, who directed the study. "These are kids who are good at recruiting a substitute parent who is a good model for them."[7]

Lifetime Relationships Increase Our Resources

To paraphrase Bill Moyers: the chief reward of long-lasting relationships is the joy of learning, of coming away from each person with a wider angle of vision on the times in which we live, on the issues we are expected to act upon, and the choices we make as mothers, wives, Christians, and citizens. We need the consistent input of others to diagnose and treat our isolation and enlarge our understanding. We need others' talents, energies, and emotions on which to draw.[8]

Superficial, occasional relationships do little to add to our store of knowledge of people and this world. We need the time it takes to hear poignant memories, exchange ideas, watch principles being lived out, develop sensitivities, and pull the depth of insights out of another soul. And you never know when a friend will provide an unexpected open door of opportunity.

I met Alan Cliburn in 1977. He was teaching a class at the Mount Hermon Christian Writers Conference in California. I learned so much from him about how to market reprints, I sent a note of appreciation. He wrote back. I wrote again. We began to share tidbits and illustrations over the years about our families (and his pet squirrel) and our writing projects. A friendship grew.

When Alan met my husband, he mentioned a magazine to him that needed short stories for boys. "You may be just the type of writer they're looking for."

My husband sent a sample story. The editor liked it and asked him to send more. Soon, they asked Steve to send stories to another magazine in their company for older boys. Eventually, they asked him to write a monthly column in their magazine for dads. Then one day, the vice-president of the umbrella organization was driving down a freeway in Chicago when he heard my husband give a talk on WMBI radio entitled, "Ten Things Every Dad Ought To Do." Because he remembered Steve's name from the in-house magazine, he called with an offer. "We're just begin-

ning a series of fathering conferences all across
Would you be interested in being one of our main :

He definitely would.

That sequence evolved because an acquaintance became something more: a friend. A friend who had a resource. A friend, we hope, for life.

Lifetime Relationships Tend to Be Comfortable and Sincere

George Eliot once expounded, "Oh, the comfort, the
inexpressible comfort of feeling safe with a person; having neither to weigh thoughts nor measure words, but to
pour them all out, just as they are, chaff and grain together,
knowing that a faithful hand will take and sift them, keep
what is worth keeping, and then, with the breath of kindness, blow the rest away."[9]

We can't tell just anybody the thoughts and feelings we
have, the things we discover. Wisdom advises that we
select with whom we share our inner being. Some words
are best left for God's ears alone. But what a treasure to
find a heart that allows you to be yourself. That kind of
loyalty only happens in the crucible of the test of years.

Recently, my sister-in-law came to visit. How at ease I
felt in preparing for her stay. No frantic white glove
inspection. No trying to impress with exotic meals. No
desperate last-ditch effort to lose five pounds before her
arrival. I looked forward to the long chats I knew we
would have, like we had gradually grown to expect during
the twenty-seven years since I'd married her brother.

If I said something dumb, I knew she wouldn't get all
huffy or disown me. She'd give me another chance. Too
many experiences through the years, too much practice in
enjoying each other's company would go to waste if she
didn't.

17

Because of a social legal contract, Judy and I are now related to each other. But, by choice and effort, we have also become friends.

Lifetime Relationships Sweeten Pleasures and Soften Sorrows

"Two are better than one, because they have a good return for their work: If one falls down, his friend can help him up. But pity the man who falls and has no one to help him up!" (Eccles. 4:9, 10).

One day, my husband scooted me out the door and told me to "Get lost."

I'd been cloistered for weeks in the house with mothering, housework, and writing assignments. He couldn't stand my moaning anymore. I gladly trekked off to a nearby mountain lake with a good book, notepaper, and Sandi Patti cassettes. I spent hours under some ancient oaks refreshing my mind and spirit. Then I got hungry.

I drove to a restaurant where Steve and I had often gone. I slumped into one of our favorite back corner booths and ordered the usual: whole wheat avocado and sour cream croissant sandwich and a Diet Coke, topped off with strawberry-rhubarb parfait.

It wasn't the same. The food didn't taste as good. The scenery out the window didn't inspire me half as much. The lighting seemed dim, rather than cozy. Something was wrong. Someone was missing. I needed Steve with me.

A few weeks ago, a young wife and mother died suddenly, leaving four children and a distraught husband. At the funeral, friends counted more than a thousand mourners. One after another, they spoke of the many kindnesses this quiet, gentle woman had shown them: opening her home to confused teens, cramming her station wagon full of neighbor kids, bringing homemade soup to an ill mother's family.

"She never brought attention to herself" was repeated over and over.

She left behind a host of lifetime friends who would now be helping hands and hearts for five grieving loved ones.

Lifetime Relationships Give Meaning and Impetus to Causes

"If I have a faith that can move mountains, but have not love, I am nothing. If I give all I possess to the poor and surrender my body to the flames, but have not love, I gain nothing" (1 Cor. 13:2, 3).

Our planet is seething with injustice, perversion, and apathy. The air's polluted. Our food's cancer-causing. Fatal diseases abound. Harmful wastes are dumped in public waters and community lots. Our prisons bulge. Babies are aborted by the millions. Children are abused by those they trust. An epidemic of drugs, an explosion of pornography, and a rampage of violence flourish.

Are you bored? Does life lack meaning? Feel unneeded? No problem. Just pick a cause. There are plenty of challenges for everyone. The fire for crusading quickly fizzles, however, when there're no specific individuals for whom you toil. Hurting people keep you going.

Pat Boone gave little thought to the plight of homosexuals until a long series of letters and interactions with a former lesbian he calls "Barbara Evans."[10]

Gloria Hope Hawley found direction for her boundless energies when her concerns turned to communicating the needs of the mentally retarded to churches after the birth of her special children, Craig and Laura.[11]

Pastor David Wilkerson redirected his ministry emphasis when teenage crime in big city slums centered on the

19

transformed faces of Nicky Cruz and his friends, Angelo, Luis, and Maria.[12]

At seventeen, Amy Carmichael carried a heavy bundle for a poor Belfast woman in rags, which led her to teach classes at a mission for "shawlies" (working girls who couldn't afford hats), which led her to the rescue of temple children in India and fifty-five more years of service to the poor.[13]

Flesh and blood concerns spark true mercy and compassion and motivate deeds that are unselfish and effective.

Lifetime Relationships Help Us Obey God

"Religion that God our Father accepts as pure and faultless is this: to look after orphans and widows in their distress and to keep oneself from being polluted by the world" (James 1:27).

God studies our relationships to test the sincerity of our devotion to him. Orphans and widows. Mother and father. Husband and children. Neighbors and strangers. Even enemies. They're all a mirror reflecting the measure of how much we practice what he has preached.

Bill Tamplin ran off with another woman during a drunken binge. Now he wants another chance.

"As long as he keeps going to the counselor, I have hope that we can work things out," his wife, Stephany, says. "People keep telling me to forget him, that he'll never change. They even try to fix me up with dates. It's slow going right now; but I believe, with God's help, I can learn to love him again. When I said, 'till death do us part,' I meant it."

Genevieve had gotten Sonja a job at the huge retail dressmakers where she worked as a bookkeeper. A year later, Sonja disappeared and so did thousands of dollars out of the vault in Genevieve's office.

"I pray for her every day," Genevieve confided to her co-workers. "She has to have some desperate needs to have done such a thing to me."

A few weeks later, Sonja gave herself up and returned most of the money. Genevieve was one of her most frequent visitors in jail.

Patsy and Marilyn had been good friends for several years. Suddenly, Marilyn became distant toward Patsy. After a few embarrassing attempts at breaking through this facade, Patsy was tempted to ignore Marilyn and find a new friend.

"But I knew she meant more to me than that," Patsy explained. "I wrote her a note explaining how I treasured our friendship and didn't understand what was bothering her. She called me and tearfully blurted out that a story she had told me in strict confidence had been repeated by me during a Bible study.

"I was devastated. She was right. I didn't realize how telling the story to others would hurt her. If I hadn't gone to the trouble of writing to her, this wound may have festered forever. I would have lost a lifetime friend. Now I have the tough job of proving she can trust me again."

Stephany. Genevieve. Patsy. Each of these women struggled that extra mile in their strained relationships because of their love for God and their willingness to read and obey his instructions for living.

Lifetime Relationships Ease the Stress of Growing Older

Samuel Johnson wrote, "If a man does not make new acquaintances as he advances through life, he will soon find himself left alone. A man, Sir, should keep his friendships in constant repair."[14]

Casey Morgan will never know a lonely moment. At

age seventy-three, she's still spry and working on relationships, old ones as well as new. When we moved to town, she stopped by for a neighborly visit. "I want to know all about you," she said. "I'm nosy that way from my newspaper reporting days."

Later, we learned she's also the honorary town historian, keeping records of family trees for all the early pioneers in the area. A healthy curiosity and sincere interest has always kept her involved with people.

What's the difference between a seventy-year-old and herself at twenty years old?

The older woman is reaping what the younger woman sowed.

Who you are this year is an extension of what you were becoming the year before. If you don't trouble to work at friendships when you're young and healthy and chasing after dreams, you won't find it any easier when the knees begin to buckle and the gray hairs come. By then, the friends will have thinned out, too. And risking new friendships will be a rusty, awkward process, easily discouraged.

Why stretch love to last longer than a season?

Because that's what keeps us fully human.

Why make a commitment that endures the span of life?

Because that's part of what draws us into the company of the divine.

TIME TO CONSIDER

1. Describe the pattern for your present relationships. Do they tend to be long-term or short-term? Why?

2. Describe a present relationship that you hope endures for a lifetime. What will your part be to make this happen?

3. Do you miss a former relationship? How could this relationship be renewed?

4. Which means of contact do you most like to use? Least? Which do you appreciate *receiving*?

- letters
- telephone
- eating out
- gifting
- parties
- meals at home
- movies

- sports
- making gifts
- dropping by unannounced
- offering a service (baby-sitting, cleaning, etc.)
- other:_____

5. Which of the above do you think would help to strengthen a relationship that is presently faltering?

2
...

It Takes All Kinds

"He drew a circle that shut me out—
Heretic, rebel, a thing to flout.
But Love and I had the wit to win:
We drew a circle that took him in!"[1]

Can we choose the people who will be our lifelong
friends?
Yes.
And no.
We can choose to commit ourselves to another person,
regardless of their response to us.
• Because no one else cares like we do.
• Because she needs our attention, though she doesn't
recognize it yet.
• Because she needs what we have to give, but, for one
reason or another, is unable to return our love.

25

• Because we've made a promise or vow we've got to keep.

• Because God has put that person in our mind, though we can't, at the moment, figure out why.

Perhaps the notion simply never occurs to any of our acquaintances or relations that they need to pursue more than a day-to-day (or year-to-year) commitment to us. It's the "lease option" mentality for relationships. When it's not convenient anymore and a little effort is needed to keep the contact going, they'll look for someone more available. In order for them to fully buy into this relationship, a nudge is needed. That's because your contact with them probably fits into one of these five types of friendship categories:

REGIONAL

In a *regional* friendship, the only reason you ever get together is because you meet at a common place during the ordinary events of your everyday life. A shared piece of geography, a space of land during a measured period of time—that's the only pact that binds you together. You live in the same neighborhood, you work in the same office, you attend the same class. Or she's your hair dresser; he's your grocery clerk. Perhaps you met on an ocean cruise, at summer camp, or she lives next door to your parents' beach cabin. Little or no more contact is made, though you seem compatible or interested in one another's activities when you visit.

Karla Bence tells of the wonderful friendship she shared with Dorothea. They met at a flea mart and, as they talked, realized they had a lot of the same needs. Both faced their first year as pastors' wives. Both were pregnant with their first child. Their husbands served churches that had come through similar difficult experiences. Because they lived in neighboring towns, they set up a monthly appointment at a nearby beach or restaurant. This lasted three years. Then both of their husbands transferred.

"We've never seen each other since. We don't even write. Strange . . ." Karla comments, "after all those personal things we shared with each other."

Karla and Dorothea made an extra push to see each other; but in the end, their relationship comes under the heading of *regional*. That's all they required of each other. That's all they gave.

MUTUAL-PARTNERSHIP

Showing horses for dressage. Weekly appointments at the health club. Scouring auctions together for pieces of unchipped carnival, ruby, and depression glass. Searching the skies with the astronomy club for meteor showers and visible planets. Playing on the women's softball team.

With a common interest or activity, friendship blossoms. It can quickly wither, if untended, when the activity no longer brings you together.

At one time, I discovered that all my relationships were neatly organized into boxes: My writing friends. My church friends. The Toastmaster buddies, the night school classmates, and the concert series companions. I never made any effort to include one group, either through conversation or invitation, into the other parts of my life. Separate. Safe. Compartmentalized.

Imagine my shock when Sherry exposed the same kind of thinking and I realized what we were all missing.

Sherry arrived at the Gershwin concert ecstatic, hyper, and hardly able to keep quiet long enough to listen to the prelude. When I pressed her to explain her exuberance, she blurted out, "Robbie's been healed! We've been praying for five years, and the doctors finally found an antibiotic that works!"

I did know that Robbie was their eleven-year-old son, but I had no idea that he suffered a chronic illness or even that Sherry was a Christian. I couldn't have told you before that night what church she attended. We only discussed music and side topics that related to music. Until that moment, the friendship never dipped deeper than the *mutual-partnership* level.

DORMANT

The *dormant* relationship begins by a shared experience that touches your emotions. At one particular season of your life, together you faced a challenge that was either exhilarating, devastating, or poignant in some way.

This could be:

• wartime
• political campaigns
• natural disasters
• walking the picket lines
• serving on the pastor-seeking committee
• coping with similar illness or injury

Depending on how long a time the interaction took place and the rapport you established, these relationships can instantly come alive again after a lengthy parting of the ways. You feel as if you've never been separated. The shared experience impacted you much more than if you had a mere regional or mutual-partnership past. This type of relationship can also bloom when the common thread in the past was not necessarily an experience you endured together.

Carol Burnett and Julie Andrews, entertainment stars, took to each other immediately when they met in 1961. "We went to a Chinese restaurant after my show," Carol recalls, "and we didn't stop talking. I felt as if we'd known each other for years. No one else could get a word in edgewise."

They realized later their instant affinity had a lot to do with similar emotional backgrounds. "We're both adult children of alcoholics," Carol explains. "We both grew up with the same kinds of needs and insecurities. . . . Because we've gone through so many similar situations as women—as wives and mothers and professionals—our understanding is almost instinctive."

Though their careers have kept them much apart, whenever they meet again, such as working on a show together, the special feelings for each other are revived. A hardship in common as children has bonded them together as adults.[2]

INVESTMENT-TUTOR

This can be a strictly one-sided relationship, at least for a time. One person sees potential in another and invests time and effort in training or companionship, without any signs of initial gratitude, attention, or love returned.

Teaching is like that. Sometimes, so is parenting. Perhaps a marriage endured during difficult conditions falls into this arrangement.

A friendship can also evolve this way.

Alison McHenry lives miles out of town in the desert of central Nevada. Her husband's a cattle rancher and prospector. He's gone much of the year. Alison's three children live east of the Missouri, and she can't drive because of an ailment. Many of her daytime hours she spends doped by medicine and depressed, watching soap operas and game shows on TV. At night, she reads romance novels.

Merilee Blanchard resides in California now, but she once lived close to Alison. They met at the doctor's office when they were both being treated for skin cancers. Merilee writes to Alison about once a month, sending recipes and pictures and family stories and articles she thinks Alison might like. She keeps on writing, even though Alison only scrawls out a line or two at Christmas in reply.

"The Lord gave her to me for some reason," Merilee explains. "She's one of my appointed people."

MUTUAL-NURTURE

In the *mutual-nurture* relationship, both individuals value the presence of the other, giving time and attention to all the small and large details that allow love to breathe and develop. They enhance one another's most attractive traits. They refuse to allow distance or problems or a multitude of other friendships to diminish the depth of their commitment to, and enjoyment of, each other.

This describes some of the best marriages and the most delightful kinships, both within and without the family unit. Said Anne Shirley, the winsome orphan of *Anne of Green Gables*, "I must find a bosom friend—an intimate friend—a really kindred spirit to whom I can confide my inmost soul."[3]

Our friend, Rod, owned a western-wear store a few miles down the road from the city. It was more or less a "mom and pop" operation, with a couple of longtime employees. Then Rod got a chance to move up to the big time. A huge shopping center was going in downtown in the high rent district. A businessman whom Rod had known for years wanted him to become a partner in an ambitious new store in the mall.

Rod jumped at the chance. After all, the kids were in high school, and soon college bills, weddings, and all that would be coming. After several delays and countless trips to the bankers, attorneys, and accountants, they signed a wagonload of documents.

After a rush of sales the first two weeks, the business began to flounder. Rod soon ran out of clientele interested in wearing boots and cowboy hats. But the daily stress of overhead and inventory costs remained. Rod wasn't used to this kind of pressure.

His partner continued to wheel and deal. He secured another sizable loan from the bank and assured Rod that the Christmas season would get them in the black.

It didn't.

On December 29, Rod's partner decided he would rather live in the South Pacific supported by most of the bank loan.

By February 1, the new store folded. By March 1, Rod's original store and his spacious five-bedroom ranch house were taken over by the lending institution.

Rod was devastated. He blamed himself. "I was too greedy for gain to investigate this guy more," he admitted.

Now Rod, Nancy, and the kids live in an apartment next to the city park. He works as a clerk for a hardware store. Nancy keeps books for an insurance company. If their oldest finds a part-time job, he can go to a community college in September.

A glowing inspiration remains in all of this to those of us who have watched them. His wife, Nancy, lets everyone know she still thinks Rod is the greatest guy on earth. She initiates social times with their friends. She tags along with him as they bounce from attorneys to courtrooms to criminal investigations. She is by his side at basketball games, church meetings, and at the supermarket.

Not once has anyone heard her complain about having to give up the house or the business and start over.

Rod may have lost nearly everything else in the world, but he still has his best friend.[4]

WHERE DO I BEGIN?

There's no bad place to start.

Any of the relationships described above have the potential, with cultivation, of progressing to the *mutual-nurture* level.

However, that isn't necessarily the desired result in every case, because we don't have the energy and focus required to develop more than a limited number of relationships to the *mutual-nurture* level.

Even so, rich relationships can happen within all the other categories, even kept to their confining boundaries, such as the *regional* or *mutual-partnership* if long-term effort is exerted. We need the opportunities for giving and receiving sincere human exchange that each of these types of friendship offer. They widen opportunities for expanding lifetime relationships, with a broadened potential for influencing many friends for Christ and giving and receiving encouragement when life gets tough. After all, the people you know—by face, by name, by shared experiences—can best reach your heart and change your will.

Any *mutual-nurture* relationship insures a lifetime commitment, unless it's allowed to regress to one of the other stages. All that's required is watchful care by both parties. Each of the other types could be a possible lifetime pursuit, without the *mutual-nurture* depth of intimacy, and still accomplish satisfying opportunities for unselfish giving of yourself.

Few, if any, of your relationships should be left to shift for themselves, with no vision for them except what you can see for the moment's pleasure and convenience. The rest of this book will cover role model examples, principles, and projects that could propel your temporary alliances into permanent bonds.

TIME TO CONSIDER

1. List the five categories of relationships given in this chapter. Put names of three acquaintances that fit the description under each heading.

2. Place a check by those you'd like to consider for a lifelong, rather than a short-term, friendship.

3. Have you become too isolated? Are your relationships so narrow that all the people on your list think like you, act like you, talk like you, look like you? If so, what could you do to broaden the variety of people you allow into your intimate circle?

4. Mother Teresa, nurse to the poor of Calcutta, isn't a woman who judges others. The harshest comment she ever makes about even the most villainous person is that she has met "Jesus in a *very* distressing disguise." Does anyone on your list fit this portrayal? If so, ask God for wisdom in handling this relationship.

5. What could you do today to let one of the people on your list know you care about them?

3
...

How Come I Still Don't Like Me?

I shied into the peopled room,
  Alone.

The only one I knew
  was me.

And why did I feel
(at once)
so large
so loud
so small
  so ME

  yet no one
    noticed.[1]

35

What factor most prevents you from working on and expanding your relationships?
- Time?
- Interest?
- Laziness?
- Shyness?

Or does the reason dig much deeper?
- Fear?
- Mistrust?
- Bitter memories?
- Insecurity?

Many of us struggle with crippling inner weaknesses that hamper our ability to reach out to other humans.

Once I asked a group of women, "What one thing is still your greatest struggle in life?"

A few scattered replies buzzed around the room: "Being a good wife and mother." "Knowing whether to work or not." "Finding time to read my Bible and pray."

Shelley, an attractive and talented leader in the group, hesitated at first, then raised her hand. "I've read many books the last few years on self-image, and some have helped. But I don't understand—how come I still don't like me?" Her face flushed crimson as she glanced nervously around the room.

One by one, the other women nodded in agreement. Encouraged, Shelley added, "It can be so depressing— I'm too afraid to attempt anything, even for the Lord, when I battle questions like: 'How do I look today?' 'How come so-and-so isn't speaking to me?' 'How come I can't do anything right?' Can I ever get past this stage?"

Mary Ellen responded, "I have days like that, too. I'm so self-conscious, so sensitive about myself and what others are thinking, that I can't relate well to people. Sometimes it happens during my monthly cycle. Other times it happens when I've been mulling over a bad scene, like when my sister forgot my birthday. I bring back all the old hurts from the past, and soon I've got a full-blown depression."

I jumped on Mary Ellen's comment about the inability to relate to people. "When you're caught up with yourself, it's hard to care about what's going on in the lives of others?"

"Yeah," said Christine, a mother of two teens. "I just want to be off alone somewhere and sulk about life's injustices."

Shelley sighed and confessed as she tried to hold back tears, "You guys make it sound as if it's a temporary phase you go through. I feel this way all the time."

Later, Shelley and I talked more. "My mother died when I was just twelve. For years before that, she'd been so ill she couldn't give me much attention. My father tried to raise me and my brother, but he never could say anything good about me. He still can't. No matter what I do, there's never any praise, any recognition, only criticism for how I could do better. I long for one sincere, honest word of appreciation from him. I think it affects my friendships. I always pick friends who tell me how much they admire me. When the relationship settles into a normal routine, I tire of it and pick out someone else."

How different is Nancy Prowell's experience. "I can honestly say I never felt like a nobody," she said. "I was born into a wonderful, close-knit family. My father was a minister, and we didn't have a lot of earthly possessions. However, we kids were taught that we didn't need to be beautiful, wealthy, or outstanding in many areas, that we were created individually for a purpose, and that we were important to God. My parents passed this on to us, and I am thankful."

Nancy had a long, full marriage with her husband. They

were childless, so she heaped her love on her many nieces and nephews and felt no regrets. Widowed in later life, she remarried and took on the responsibility of helping raise several teenage stepchildren. "I appreciate any kindness they show me," she explains, "and understand when they let me know their real mother is still first in their hearts. We have tense times, but I enjoy this chance to help them through their sorrow."

Nancy found a base in her childhood home for the gracious art of lifetime relationships.

The words and actions of important people in your life as you grew up strongly affect your view of yourself and others. Dr. James Dobson says, "Often the greatest damage is unintentionally inflicted right in the home, which should be the child's sanctuary and fortress."[2]

To show love if we've never been given love is difficult. Babies aren't born with the ability to love. They must be cuddled and hugged and cooed, or they'll die, either physically or emotionally. As a child grows older, he or she needs to see love in action, to watch how love works.

God designed parents to be models of practical everyday love to their children. In years past, the church and secular society depended on the laboratory of the family to teach children the basics of social relationships. Those dependable commitments provided a solid social structure and wholesome development for the individual personality. But with marriage and parenting bonds disintegrating, many children and those adults who are still emotionally needy children inside must find their sources of teaching about and receiving love elsewhere. Children today are growing up in "the school of conditional relationships."[3]

Our ability, or inability, to commit ourselves to a lifetime relationship is often a product of how we were raised or what we have been conditioned to think about ourselves.

If the negative is true for you or someone you're trying to befriend, *there's still a way out*. The road may be much rockier as you battle the habits of the years, but loving other people can still be learned.

Everyone has a problem with selfishness. But some live so much inside themselves, they either fume with self-hatred or foam over with self-adulation. Both tendencies lessen the chances for maintaining lifetime relationships. How can you tell if you're prone to either of these excesses?

SELF-EXAMINATION VERSUS SELF-CENTEREDNESS

Self-examination is good—perhaps at the end of a day or a week or a year. The Bible says we're all born sinners, that is, without God's help we can do nothing truly good (see 1 John 1:8, Isaiah 64:6, and John 15:5). Even when we trust God's Son, Jesus, as our Savior from this sinful, selfish inner nature, we must be constantly on the alert not to fall back into those old patterns of thinking and doing. Living like Jesus takes lifelong practice. That's why Christians aren't instantly perfect. God takes each child of his through a thorough, individually designed training process.

Those who engage in healthy self-examination ask questions like:

• "Whom have I wronged recently? What can I do about it?"

• "What harmful thoughts am I indulging in? How will I change this habit?"

• "Whom have I neglected lately? When will I show them I really care?"

• "Which of my actions or words irritate other people? How and when will I work to change?"

This kind of personal interrogation prepares you for a

right relationship with God and a willingness to make peace with people. A woman with a proper view of who she is, and who she is not, makes the best relationships. This is a definition of a humble person, the type of individual everyone likes to be around.

You can also quickly discern the cesspool of *self-centeredness*. Those with an inordinate preoccupation with themselves find their every waking thought caught in these futile cycles:

- "What are they thinking about me?"
- "Why didn't she smile or speak when we passed?"
- "Why don't I have the same opportunities they have?"
- "Why can't I ever do anything with my hair?"
- "I can't possibly take on that responsibility; I don't have anything to wear!"
- "Why don't they ever give me what I need?"

Obsessive pecking at yourself distorts your view of yourself and others. People are seen only as reflections of how they respond to you. You assume they are as dreary inside as you are. An honest interchange with another human isn't possible while you're trapped in the abyss of endless speculations and anxieties.

When you find yourself sucked into self-centered imaginings, one of the best antidotes is to initiate an act of kindness in a surprising new direction for you. Perhaps that will be to

- a stranger you meet in the grocery store
- an elderly person in a convalescent home
- a neighbor you've tended to ignore
- a widow at your church
- a child who has always bugged you
- an unusual aunt who never fit in with the rest of the family
- the woman who's always trying to borrow something

• the editor who wrote nasty things about your favorite singer

• the mother who refused to help with the classroom party

• the strange old man who's hard to understand

• the family who lost everything in a fire.

What does an act of kindness look like?

• lending a lawn mower

• giving away your extra winter coat

• saying, "I'm sorry"

• tears

• a pot of homemade soup

• a glass of icy lemonade

• a clean bed at a moment's notice

• a visit to the local prison or juvenile hall

• a hand on the shoulder

• a "fun food" package

• saying, "Let's start this all over again."

Ted Engstrom, president emeritus of World Vision International, tells a simple story of how his wife, Dorothy, began a lifelong relationship. The day before Thanksgiving, she went to the store for one item: a jar of cranberries. Only one jar sat on the shelf. As she reached for it, so did another woman.

"In the spirit of the season, each insisted the other take the jar. Finally, the manager of the store intervened and said there were more cranberries in the back room. Dorothy proceeded to give her new friend, Bette, one of her favorite recipes for a pink and fluffy cranberry sherbet. After the holidays, the two women got together. Before long, even Bette's husband, Ned, would stop by the house just to talk." Through Dorothy's friendship, Bette and her whole family, including five children, have come to trust in Jesus Christ.[4]

Friends Forever

No one on earth can ever claim they've never been loved. No individual, believer or nonbeliever, saint or sinner, has ever been far from the love God pours into our world every day. Yes, we're surrounded by evil and havoc on every side—a quick look at the newspaper or ears open down at the post office proves that. But God's love and power still restrains the full brunt of the horrors possible, while he allows human rebellion to run its course.

If you've been denied the joy of faithful, committed human love during critical turning points in your life and that prevents you from risking relationships, *draw upon the full measure of the love of God readily available to you.*

"And I pray that you, being rooted and established in love, may have power, together with all the saints, to grasp how wide and long and high and deep is the love of Christ, and to know this love that surpasses knowledge" (Eph. 3:17-19).

Shelley, who challenged our discussion group with her questions about liking herself, in time discovered one of her main problems. She had a faulty view of God. Perhaps her relationship with her father hampered her trust in her heavenly Father.

"As I've studied the Bible in this class," she told us one day, "I've realized that I can't imagine God being sensitive enough or caring enough to handle my fears and doubts. I picture him either as a somewhat ferocious giant in the sky or as an aloof administrator. But when I read about him as a tender, loving, all-wise Father—well, I'd like to have the nerve to go sit in his lap awhile."

Shelley learned, in effect, to do just that. In getting to know God better, she was surprised to discover her low self-image didn't entirely disappear. When a human reaches out to a holy God, one's own sinful nature becomes clearer. This is a necessary step in becoming a spiritual person and

42

in showing compassion and sensitivity to the many imperfect people around you.

The more we see God as he is, the more we will see ourselves as we are. A low or negative self-image may be necessary before we understand our need for God. The Bible presents a striking example of this phenomenon. The prophet Isaiah "saw the Lord seated on a throne, high and exalted" (Isa. 6:1). This incredible sight caused Isaiah to cry out, "Woe to me! . . . I am ruined. For I am a man of unclean lips" (Isa. 6:5).

When Isaiah witnessed firsthand the glory of God, he cringed at what he saw in himself.

Then Isaiah's attention was drawn to the faults of the people around him. "I live among a people of unclean lips" (Isa. 6:5). He wasn't the only one—everyone else was messed up, too!

Isaiah escaped this miserable helplessness (his utter sinfulness and the sinfulness of the people around him) by instantly accepting God's offered forgiveness and peace. Now he could stand clean, worthy, and forgiven before God. "Then one of the seraphs flew to me with a live coal in his hand, which he had taken with tongs from the altar. With it he touched my mouth and said, 'See, this has touched your lips; your guilt is taken away and your sin atoned for' " (Isa. 6:6, 7).

When Isaiah saw himself as he really was, he was shocked, mortified. He thought he might as well die; he was no earthly (or heavenly) good. He saw everyone else that way, too. Who wants to befriend (or in Isaiah's case, serve) people as worthless and wretched as you are? Isaiah's self-esteem was shattered, making him ready to grab hold of God's unconditional love and offer of a new, fresh start. He knew that if he could be this bad and God still wanted him, anyone had hope. God softened Isaiah's

43

attitude toward people, even while he admitted the truth of their potential rottenness. Otherwise, Isaiah would never be able to endure the commitment to the rigorous mission God planned for him.

Do you have to like yourself before you're willing or able to like other people?

Or by forcing yourself to reach out to others, do you learn how to like yourself?

It can work both ways.

But, like Isaiah, somewhere in the process, God wants his say. He knows you better than anyone else possibly could. He knows why you may have difficulty with long-term relationships.

He knows what is needed to change this deficiency in you.

A lifetime of a wide diversity of satisfying relationships requires the help of a Master teacher, one who'll be with you for the long run—every day that you live.

TIME TO CONSIDER

1. Read Romans 12:3. How do you see yourself? Do you tend to assess yourself too high, too low, or just about right? Share your answer with a friend. Does she agree with your assessment?

2. "It may be possible for each to think too much of his own potential glory hereafter; it is hardly possible for him to think too often or too deeply about that of his neighbor."[5]

Consider the above quote. How would you describe the general inward atmosphere of your feelings toward other people? Pick out the closest word from the list below:

___ judgment   ___ fear

___ trust   ___ caution

44

___ apathy   ___ impatience
___ interest   ___ compassion
___ acceptance   ___ nervousness
___ care   ___ other _____
___ suspicion

Are you content with this emotional climate? If not, why not?

3. Describe a time when you felt unlovely or unlovable. Who helped to lift you out of this pit? How did they do it? Is someone you know going through a similar experience? If so, how might you help her?

4. Dr. James Dobson claims four common barriers can cause a child to doubt his or her own worth. Do any of these strike a chord in your own experience?
• parental insensitivity
• fatigue and time pressure
• guilt
• rivals for love[6]
If so, how?

5. Are you the type of person you would choose for a lifetime friend? Why, or why not?

6. What's the difference between having a poor self-image and recognizing you're a sinner in God's eyes? Are they the same problem?

4
...
"If You Do That Once More, I'll . . ." (and Other Touchy Subjects)

Fill in the blanks for the following statements:

"I could never live with someone who_____."

"I can't stand it when anybody_____."

"I'm pretty calm most of the time, but _____ drives me up a wall."

This is how I would answer:

I could never live with someone who smokes.

I can't stand it when anybody crunches apples or smacks gum near my ears.

I'm pretty calm most of the time, but constant whining and complaining drive me up a wall.

What does this say about me? Well, you now have formerly private information that could enable you to torture me effectively, should you so desire. You also know where my defenses break down in my desire to

47

establish and maintain lifetime relationships. Since I have no power to change the habits of another person, I will either have to eliminate anyone who smokes, crunches apples, smacks gum or whines from my list of "people who I can like on a long-term basis" or call upon more reserves, resources, ingenuity, and love within myself for folks who do such things.

The Bible is full of narratives of people countering the irritable habits of the people they try to love.

Rachel and Leah were sisters, both married to Joseph because of their father's deceit. Joseph really loved Rachel, but he was stuck with Leah, too. Jealousy and competition caused friction in the household. Leah couldn't stand to see *Joseph's fawning over Rachel*. Rachel resented *Leah's fertility*. Every pregnancy set off torrents of smug digs by Leah and a season of depression for Rachel. Rachel's response was to gripe to her husband: "Give me children, or I'll die!" (see Genesis 29 and 30).

Miriam, the sister of Moses, had many strong qualities. She shielded her brother when his life was threatened as a baby. She was a teacher. She had a patriotic vision for her people. She was the first woman singer on record. She was a commanding figure in the celebration of the Israelites after their miraculous escape through the Red Sea. But something really bugged her. That is, someone. She didn't care for Moses' wife, a Cushite woman from *a different race and background*. Her foreign ways rankled Miriam, which needled her into public criticism of her brother, now a great leader of hundreds of thousands of wandering people. Miriam's envious, bitter side began to show (see Numbers 12).

Hannah faced an almost identical situation as Rachel. Her husband, Elkanah, had another wife, Peninnah. Peninnah had children, but Hannah was barren. Because of this, Peninnah *"kept provoking her in order to irritate her."* At first, she wept to her husband about it, but finally she took the matter to God, and the situation was soon resolved (see 1 Samuel 1).

Michal, King David's wife, *couldn't stand for her husband to dance in the streets* where the common people could see him. This practice made her ashamed of him. She felt it wasn't dignified enough for a man of his (and her) position. She responded with mockery and scorn (see 2 Samuel 6:16-23).

Then there's Martha, trying to entertain Jesus with a hot homecooked meal, and she sure could use some help. Meanwhile, her sister Mary lounged at the feet of their guest, listening to his stories. Martha called it *laziness,* and she was quick to draw both Mary's and Jesus' attention to that fact. Jesus chided Martha for her mixed priorities (see Luke 10:38-42).

The Bible says that "[love] is not easily angered" (1 Cor. 13:5).

One of the unexplained ironies of human nature is the tendency for moral and otherwise good people to have outbreaks of ill temper. "The vice of the virtuous" it's been called. They're impatient, short, sharp toward the foibles of their family and friends.

"We are inclined to look upon bad temper as a very harmless weakness. We speak of it as a mere infirmity of nature, a family failing, a matter of temperament, not a thing to take into very serious account in estimating a man's character. And yet . . . the Bible again and again returns to condemn it as one of the most destructive elements in human nature."[1]

A touchy disposition can embitter life, break up communities, destroy the most sacred relationships, and devastate homes.

"She keeps asking me to come visit, but I can't be with

that woman for two minutes without screaming inside. My nerves are so on edge, I actually believe I could kill her," Carolee stormed one afternoon over tea. "The way she grinds her teeth together and flutters her eyes every word she speaks. She still insists on leading that committee. Hasn't anyone ever had the nerve to tell her how she comes across?"

"Did you know she has partial paralysis in the left side of her face from a stroke?" Carolee's mother interrupted quietly.

Carolee sucked her breath in sharply. "Ohhh, no, I didn't realize."

The next time Carolee attended a meeting with Mrs. Bennett, she was surprised to note how much easier she tolerated the woman's mannerisms. Understanding the reason behind the action put a whole new perspective on Carolee's response.

"I'd like to come see you on Thursday afternoon," she finally offered. "Could I bring my daughter, too?"

"Oh yes," Mrs. Bennett replied. "She can look at my doll collection. Of course, you know that I make ceramic dolls for the Christmas fairs."

Carolee didn't. That was just one of the many things that Carolee learned about this amazing woman, insights Carolee could have completely missed because she couldn't see past grinding teeth and fluttering eyes.

COPING TOOLS

What are some coping mechanisms we can employ to help us overlook or more easily tolerate bothersome behavior?

How can we diffuse the potential bomb of unbearable idiosyncrasies that can hamper, threaten, or destroy our relationships? Here are a few suggestions.

Ask, Do I Do This or Something Similar Myself?

How much we neglect to see our own actions is amazing.

My husband, Steve, loses his keys at least once a day. That used to bother me a lot. For one thing, I kept telling him to always put them in one designated place so he'd always know where to find them. But he wouldn't listen to me. The daily cry of "where are my keys?" when he's already late to wherever he's going sent us both scattering, no matter what other project I was immersed in. I was always prepared with my "I told you so" lecture—until I remembered that I also have a habit of misplacing things.

I wear glasses all the time, except when I'm reading. As soon as I pick up a magazine, recipe, or book, the glasses get plopped down, never to be seen again until Steve or I happen to come across them tucked behind the cookie jar, sprawled out on the guest bed, or hanging half out of a drawer. I never can explain why they wound up there and rarely recall even taking them off. This definite blind spot of mine helps me be more compassionate with the daily key marathon.

Practice Good Manners

"[Love] is not rude" (1 Cor. 13:5).

Old-fashioned etiquette like "please," "thank you," and "excuse me," used in tension-producing moments, can ease built-up steam. It's the oil that can remove the grating squeak. It's practicing gracefulness, courtesy, and sensitivity when you feel in the fire. It puts a whole new meaning on the value of politeness. It adds winsomeness and charm to any personality. It's the forgotten craft of tact.

It happened again the other night. We were playing the game, Scattergories, and one of my family members challenged my perfectly good word. When the vote was called for, everyone in the gang put thumbs down—except me. I stewed in silence until the next round. When that offending family member had their own word challenged, I voted thumbs down on a tie vote that sent them hurtling into screams of protest.

"Aha, can't take your own medicine," I preened.

"You must be kidding. Your using 'gravy' as a word for Toppings on Pizza doesn't in any way compare with my picking Heloise as an example of Notorious People."

All eyes stared at me. Was there to be a big brouhaha? Would this be the start of a crack in the peace of the Bly household? The moment of decision hung like a hummingbird poised in the air. Which way would I turn?

I discreetly coughed. "You all know that I believed that, since biscuits and gravy were listed as a popular twosome on many a menu, I assumed that someone, somewhere in the world, surely has thought to pour gravy over pizza crust. But, after some consideration, I've reached the conclusion that you're all right. That's not a common practice, so I couldn't expect you all to jump on my train of thought." My careful, very polite, backhanded apology completed, I looked around at the dear, familiar faces whom I counted as lifelong friends.

They immediately guffawed, another pet peeve of mine: laughing when I've just given a serious speech. But by now, all that politeness had cooled my temper. I joined right in.

A calm, reasoned speech gives time to regroup; to think through what you want to accomplish in the long run of life, not just the present moment; and to help you calm down.

"The art of politeness cannot be learned exclusively from books of etiquette; it comes from within; it is inspired by sympathy and is guided by consideration for the feelings of others."[2]

Sometimes we're irritated by what appears a minor episode because we're edgy that this is one more put down in a long series of slights. We're really upset about something else, but this nuisance has become the match that lights the accumulated rubbish that's now kindling. We want to strike out and retaliate. There's a better way. Only the loveless take the blunt, brutal approach.

Initiate Change

Go for a walk.

Find an alternative activity to get your mind off the annoyance.

If the radio's blaring their kind of music, suggest it be turned down a bit and that you trade stations every hour or so. Or wear earplugs.

If this is a chronic problem, call a professional, a counselor, when you desperately need to shed new light on how to handle this; or a serviceman, if some mechanical difficulty has come between you.

You have a choice. This nuisance can keep you in a constant turmoil, bothered and bewildered, producing a static state that helps no one. Or this can be the stimulus for a positive, creative change.

First, think through one aggravation that tests your mettle. How do you usually react? How would you rather behave? Second, determine an entirely different response. Keep practicing this response, before and during the situation, until it comes naturally. Don't be discouraged by momentary failures. Keep trying. This puts you in control of the situation, rather than relegating you to be a mere bystander or victim. As Robert Schuller says, "If you can't solve the problem, manage it."[3]

Sometimes learning to manage "the problem" produces unexpected dividends.

Friends Forever

In the summer of 1853, an American Indian named George Crum served as chef at an elegant resort in Saratoga Springs, New York. One guest in particular complained loud and long about chef Crum's thick-cut French-style potatoes. Several times the man sent them back with a disapproving, "They're not fit to eat! Cut them thinner!"

Thoroughly exasperated, Crum decided to rile this obnoxious guest by cutting the fries so thin and crisp he couldn't possibly pick them up with a fork. The plan backfired. The guest raved over the crispy chips. Other diners quickly requested them, too. That began an enterprise for Crum that enabled him to open his own restaurant, featuring his potato chips. Today, thin, salted, crisp potato chips are America's favorite snack food.[4]

Even though George Crum grew tired of trying to please his customer, he vented his frustration in the kitchen, with an unexpected creative result, rather than storming the dining room, which would have cost him his job.

John Claypool tells another kind of story of how his mother tried to teach him about coping:

> I remember that once, as a little boy, I came down with a terrible cold, and somehow I got the idea that, if I could run very fast from one room to another, I could get away from those germs the way I could get away from my puppy when I ran faster than he. My mother found me dashing from room to room, all out of breath; and when she discovered what I was attempting to do, she gently but wisely called me to reality. She explained that there are no spatial cures for a cold, that no matter where or how fast I went, the germs would go with me. "The sooner you quit trying to run away from it and start taking medicine for it, the quicker you will get well," she said.[5]

He learned a great truth—life is, and always will be, a process of problem solving. As soon as we overcome one, another comes along. Our only option is to learn how to cope, not whether we will or not.

If we shut people out of our lives because they rub us wrong and never give those relationships a chance through creative problem solving, we've missed the point of what relationships are all about.

Tell Them Kindly What Bothers You

And ask if something about you bothers them.

That second part is essential. Especially if you want this relationship to endure past your mention of the first part.

I did some confronting of my own the other day; I approached my son with what I considered perfect mothering control. "Aaron," I said sweetly. "You're late for bed. Again."

"I know, Mom," he said. "But it's all your fault."

"Oh?" I said sternly. "How do you figure that?"

"You didn't give me a five-minute reminder and the Orange Julius I asked for never got blended and the shade in my room's not pulled down and a big spider is in my bathtub."

"Oh," I responded meekly. Gathering confidence again, I replied, "This is your five-minute reminder. You get ready for bed; I'll do the rest."

See how easy it is sometimes? You express your concern. They reply with what's bothering them. You both work at cooperation. Even with a ten-year-old, we need to hear the other side of the pet peeve spiel.

Remembering to listen will help you add that essential touch of graciousness to your relationships.

NINE SIGNS THAT I'M A GRACIOUS FRIEND

1. I accept their apologies without further discussion.
2. I know their worst faults yet still enjoy their company.
3. When they visit, I make allowances for their dislikes (such as putting cats in the garage, leaving the mushrooms out of the stroganoff, avoiding telling "fat lady" jokes).
4. I don't keep harping after they've made a decision with which I disagree.
5. I try hard to let them know their presence is not an intrusion.
6. I quickly tell them when they've done something I appreciate.
7. I give them a chance to explain how they see a situation that bothers me.
8. I don't pout or stew in silence; I let them know *why* I'm upset.
9. I'm glad when they succeed and truly sorry when they fail.

COMBATING TUNNEL VISION

Sometimes the flaws of others so engulf our attention that we see the whole person as one ghastly mistake. We categorize them as a huge messy blot on this clean, pure earth. If it weren't for this creature—this blind, self-centered, pigheaded blob who won't change so our life could be pleasant and normal like everyone else's—we'd have no trouble making and keeping lifetime relationships.

Makes one wonder, though. Do we cause others despair and anxiety because of some failing they see in us? We'd be quick to say, "Of course, I know I have my faults." But can we face the fact that all of us have at least one fatal flaw that can drive someone we care about to tears or worse? Something we're not aware of, like bad breath or knuckle-cracking?

Would we want another person to be so caught up in that one defect that they think that's all we are? Wouldn't we want them to know all the wonderful, fascinating, incredibly warm parts of our being, so they could keep our friendship potential in perspective?

Love that lasts a lifetime is gracious.

TIME TO CONSIDER

1. How do you usually cope with irritations? Has this been effective or ineffective?

2. Relate any creative ways you have learned for tolerating people's habits.

3. Read 1 Corinthians 10:13 in at least two translations. How does this verse relate to dealing with relationships?

4. Recently I overheard two women talking. One explained that an acquaintance of hers needed a lung transplant to live. "Is or was she a smoker?" her companion asked. "Yes," came the reply. "Then my sympathy for her flies out the window."

Think about this a moment. When do our pet peeves and irritations become excuses for lack of mercy and compassion? How can we know when we've crossed over that line?

5. God has to put up with imperfect people, too. The perfect, holy, all-knowing Lord is willing to live *inside* the spirit, mind, and heart of any sinner who calls on him. None of us is ever required to get that close to another human. How can he possibly bear it? How does realizing this alter your toleration level?

5
...
Somebody, Help! I'm So Angry!

Anger is a weapon.

Anger can defend a righteous cause on behalf of those we care about, or it can be aimed *at* people, used to mow them down.

It can also be a prod.

If we didn't have the capacity for anger, we'd be passionless, incapable of righting any wrongs.

Sometimes we, or the people we love, are the victims of injustice. Then we can release the energies of anger in "actions . . . that achieve the purposes for which God put anger into man's emotional makeup."[1]

A grass roots organization such as Mothers Against Drunk Drivers (M.A.D.D.) is an example of anger that translated into positive action. The key question: who benefits? Are we just spewing pent-up emotions? Or are our energies channeled into finding solutions to a problem?

When the precious or sacred is taken lightly, anger's white heat can purify. Anger can be just. But the Bible warns that all kinds of human anger must be handled with caution and control.

"My dear brothers, take note of this: Everyone should be quick to listen, slow to speak and slow to become angry, for man's anger does not bring about the righteous life that God desires" (James, 1:19, 20).

" 'In your anger do not sin': Do not let the sun go down while you are still angry, and do not give the devil a foothold" (Eph. 4:26, 27).

The home, where we're most likely to be sloppy with our manners and our feelings, also provides a breeding ground for anger.

We lash out in anger when we've been denied something.

Joyce slams the door behind her husband. She mutters and stews all day as she makes halfhearted attempts to complete her chores. By the time her husband walks in the door that evening, Joyce's gripe has reached fever pitch. She throws a frozen pizza on the kitchen counter and storms out of the house to go to her bowling league game.

What's gotten Joyce so riled? She wanted one more purchase on the credit card.

We vent our displeasure when someone or something interferes with the controls we want on our lives.

Cindy walks into her bedroom to find her three-year-old mangling her jewelry. "Trish!" she screams. "How many times have I told you to stay out of this room!" In total frustration, Cindy swats the girl and sends her reeling. She hadn't planned to spend thirty extra minutes of her already busy day untangling necklaces and chains. Her right to privacy has also been violated.

Anger springs up as a defense for pride of who we think we are or who we used to be.

Dawn yells at Tammy's umpire. She insists her daughter got home safe. Dawn considers Tammy a good runner, just like she had been. Though Tammy tries her best, she runs like a bobby-soxer, not a pro.

To learn from anger is possible. Alec did. "We had a beautiful marriage and our children yet to raise. She just walked out. She said she didn't want the responsibility anymore. Sometimes it all hits me. I struggle with the anger."

Alec is finding victory. He's finding it by *looking at his life from God's point of view.*

"I knew I still loved her, even though she'd hurt me so much. Through this devastation, I realized I loved her enough to want God's best for her, whether she came back to us or not."

Alec continued: "Slowly, I worked through my ragged emotions by praying that she'd come to know God again and find his peace—even if it meant finding it with another man. The release of anger and bitterness I experienced has helped me be a better father to our children and a better friend to her. When she visits the children, we're able to talk, and, sometimes, even laugh together. Before, I only wanted to get even by hurting her."

Alysson has a different story. She realized *her anger was a mirror of her true self.*

"At times, I just have to get out of the house," Alysson said. "Coping with kids all day long, every day, gets on my nerves. After an hour by myself, I return to sanity and find God's peace. Without those breaks, I don't know what I'd do."

She explains further: "God was telling me something. I was single for a number of years before I married. Though I was independent and selfish, I considered myself good-natured, easy to get along with. My husband and my children turned on a light to the dark side of me. I now know I need to yield myself to God at this vulnerable place. My anger had become a defense mechanism to avoid facing my weaknesses."

Alysson rightly sensed that *anger can announce a person's need for a break from a situation.*

A walk around the block, a visit to a friend, time in a separate room, working in the yard, or running an errand may be the needed diversion. If you've been struggling with a long-term inner condition, to the point that your friends think of you as an "angry person," a more drastic change of scenery may be required, along with counseling.

LOOKING AT YOUR ANGER

Before you can cope with anger, two important steps are necessary:
- Admit a problem with anger.
- Acknowledge the specific form your anger takes.

Take a look at the statements below. Check those that sound most like you (in public words or private thoughts) when someone rubs you the wrong way.

___ "If you come one step closer, I'll slap you so hard you'll wonder what hit you."

___ "Oh, I wish you wouldn't do that. It ruins my whole day."

___ "I don't care if I ever see you again."

___ "I wish you were dead."

___ "How dare you think you can do that to me!"

___ "You never were good at anything, and you never will be!"

___ "What will I do if I see her today? I'm not ready. She makes me so nervous. I'll probably say something dumb, and then I'll be madder than ever."

___ "Why can't he show the least consideration for my feelings? After all these years, you'd think he would understand me. But, no, the same tired scene is played over and over."

___ "Just wait until I'm asked to do something for them. See how they like the tables turned."

___ "Huh? I did not do that. Why do I always get blamed?"

Now, take a look at the *actions* below. Which best describes your reaction when you think you've taken all you can handle?

___ a glare	___ sharp words
___ a quick retort	___ recalling past
___ a stormy exit	offenses
___ a sarcastic remark	___ pursed lips
___ a pouting lip	___ ignoring everyone
___ throwing an object	___ hiding in front of
___ hitting something or	the TV or in a book
someone	___ running away
___ screaming	

Finally, a double-check. Take the above-marked actions and statements to several friends or family members. Do they agree with your assessment?

Recognizing and dealing with anger is essential for anyone serious about lifetime relationships.

Myrna came to that conclusion.

"It hit us hard." Myrna sighed. "Mom died. Her will was read, and everyone's upset. My sister's not talking to my brother because he inherited the car and jewelry. Dad's on edge because he lost Mom. I've got all the work to do. We seem to live in a constant state of anger."

Myrna was shocked to discover that *her family's conflicts centered around a lack of gratitude.*

"We're thinking only about what we've lost, rather than being thankful for what we had for so many years—and what we *still* have with each other."

Myrna couldn't change the others; she could only try to change herself. She decided to reverse the damaging trend by thanking God each day for the privilege of caring for the remaining family members and any other delights he brought to her attention. She prayed that God's love and peace reach each family member. The atmosphere of that home improved dramatically within weeks.

Anger-prone people can be transformed when they begin to receive all of life, including the worst of it, with a sense of gratitude. When, in the midst of a crisis, we can give thanks to God, we're developing self-control, the cream of qualities admired by humans. This attitude acknowledges "that God is good, that he who gives us our lives not only rules over us but loves us, likes us, is for us and not against us . . . [we] receive the events of life . . . as expressions of mysterious love rather than as acts of hostility. . . . Instead of seeing [difficulties] as hopeless obstacles to our happiness, we come to see them as the challenges that give life its meaning and excitement."[2]

Anger can reveal a:
- faulty view of life
- needed area of inner change
- lack of gratitude

Anger can also be a habit.

My husband could always be counted on to blow up whenever something mechanical wouldn't work. He finally realized his anger came when he felt helpless, out of control. He's breaking this habit by changing his self-talk. When these inevitable breakdowns occur, we hear him say, "Now, as Jesus would say. . . ." This stops the potential tirades cold. He's making a new habit to take the old one's place.

Anger that destroys the joy available in relationships is the *anger that centers around envy*.

"Why don't you play with Dorian anymore?" I asked a young friend of mine.

"She's so stuck up!" Lisa replied. "Ever since she won that Little Miss Mermaid beauty pageant, she tries to make everybody around her feel ugly and stupid. All she does is prance around. It doesn't even mean anything. All she got was some dumb suitcase."

That's the child's version of an adult replay. Most of us are prone to at least an occasional secret envy when a friend finds good fortune. When the mood turns ugly, as in Lisa's case, harmful anger is ready to tear friends apart.

Covetousness is grief because we don't have the same talent, benefit, or object that someone else has. Jealousy is fear, the anxiety of being replaced as the object of someone's affections. Competition is the desire to redouble one's efforts toward a goal because we're shamed or made insecure by another's achievements.

Envy, perhaps even more powerful, happens when "the individual feels his own self-esteem and status have been lowered by another person's achievement; and so he tries, inappropriately, to demean the other's success. Unlike competitiveness, envy is not at all therapeutic. It never spurs an individual to make his best efforts. . . . Behind envy there's usually rage, often originating in childhood."[3]

Personality types also have a bearing on how often and intensely we become angry.

Authors and counselors Tim and Bev LaHaye explain:

Sanguines display a quick, hot temper but immediately forget about it after their explosion. Cholerics possess an equally turbulent disposition but they can carry a grudge indefinitely and burst into flame all over again whenever reminded of what set them off. Melancholies, who are rarely quick-tempered, frequently indulge in revenge. Consequently, they mull things over for a long time, seething inwardly, but may or may not explode. Their pent-up emotions will distinctly inhibit their actual feelings and judgment. Phlegmatics rarely experience anger unless their secondary temperament is sufficiently strong to ignite them. (Everyone has two temperaments—a dominant one and a secondary one.)[4]

ESCAPING ANGER

When you wholeheartedly want to be free of the evils of anger, you'll do what it takes.

1. *Honestly confess what bothers you.* Talk it out with a mature friend who could advise you. Listen carefully to her feedback. Write out your conclusions. Keep taking the matter to God.

2. *Renounce hostility.* Hostility's an action; anger's an emotion. It's one thing to experience an emotion; it's another problem when you lash out and hurt someone. Confess that the measure of satisfaction you've derived from venting hostility is perverse and mean-spirited. Choose to *subdue your hostility* and *channel or convert your emotion of anger into helpful action* determined by careful, logical thinking. Reason it out. Avoid "free-floating" anger. Study it through to a resolution.

3. *Replace anger with goodness.* Restructure your thought patterns. Try trust, rather than cynicism, when dealing with imperfect people. Pick a specific, true state-

ment that will help replace your anger with one of these: "Love, joy, peace, patience, kindness, goodness, faithfulness, gentleness, and self-control" (Gal. 5:22).

4. *Seek God's help.* You can't do it alone. The God who created you knows best how to change you. Ask him to control your angry side. Ask him to help you find ways for you to cooperate with him.

5. *Find encouragement.* Listen to others as they explain how they've learned to control anger. They are proof you're not alone in your anger and show additional ways out of the trap.

Very few people make wise decisions or show loving actions in the midst of anger. A momentary lapse could tear down years of careful building of trust and rapport. *To better handle the initial outburst of anger, try one of these alternatives:*

—Sit down. Take a couple of deep breaths. Drink a complete cup of coffee (or tea or chocolate or water or juice) and refuse to say or do anything until the cup is empty.

—During a peaceful time when you're alone, find passages from the Bible* that deal with anger. Mark them in some way so you can flip to them quickly when you sense an imminent anger attack. Better yet, memorize these passages; then you'll always have them ready and available. Depending on how angry you are, recite at least four hundred words of these passages before you respond. This not only gives you time to settle down, but can entirely redirect your thoughts.

—Walk away from the situation. Make a tape recording of the angry response you wanted to give. Set the tape aside for at least an hour. When you listen to it, be

---

* Suggested passages: Psalm 30:5; 103:8-18; Proverbs 29:22; 1 Corinthians 13; Ephesians 4:25-32; James 1:19-27.

thankful that you held your tongue. Prepare a better response. (Don't forget to erase the tape.)

—Shop for the person who offended you. Look for something you know they'd like, a perfect gift that fits your budget. Pass up all the "get even" objects (you know, like stink bombs, spray paint, cow chips, etc.).

—Recall three separate incidents when you said or did the exact same thing. Ask yourself, *How did I want the recipient to respond to me?*

Bitterness and pride can spill over into relationships when we start digging around in our anger problem. We remember and get mad all over again. These feelings shoot out to specific individuals. Combating anger requires not only self-control, but forgiveness. Like Job in the Bible, who prayed for his unhelpful friends who made him feel worse when he was already down, we must ask God to help us forgive the people who hurt us. Otherwise, anger will keep spewing, poisoning people who had nothing whatsoever to do with the original offense.

REACH FOR A WORTHY GOAL

Anger can be good or bad.

Healthy anger searches for ways to solve the problem and drives us to destroy some evil. It seeks the welfare of others.

Spite, on the other hand, doesn't care if it harms or destroys people—others or the one it controls. All its actions create new and worse problems. Spite is counterproductive and totally selfish.

What do you really want? What's your highest priority?

Do you want to hang onto your anger?

Do you want to be known as a peaceful person?

Do you want a more pleasant, carefree existence?

Or do you want to be a caring woman—one who saves

her deepest passions for issues that are worthwhile, for people who really matter, the people you want to spend your life learning to love.

TIME TO CONSIDER

1. Think back to the last time you were angry. Did your response match the crime? What would you do differently, if you had it to do over?

What's the longest period of time you've ever been angry?

2. How do *you* deal with a person who's angry with you?

3. Read Proverbs 14:29; 16:32; and 19:11. What does the ability to control anger signify about one's character?

4. Read Proverbs 15:1 and 21:14. What are other ways to calm down a tense situation?

5. Read Hebrews 12:15 and Romans 12:19.

Of these common situations that provoke bitterness, which has been a problem for you?
- unresolved personal differences
- turning away from God
- results of sexual immorality
- watching bad people prosper
- abandoned by mate
- kids that turn out wrong
- unfair circumstances

How have you handled the problem? What has resulted?

Why do you think some people have a hard time letting go of their bitterness?

Friends Forever

Bitterness is a choice, a decision to vindicate a situation in your own way. When you give your bitterness to God, it frees you to give your best to all your relationships and it allows God the opportunity to even the score in the choicest possible way for all parties concerned.

6
...
Making the Most of Broken Relationships

Selina and I met at a home Bible study. We enjoyed digging deeper in our discussions; so after the meetings, we'd talk for hours at a local restaurant. Our fondness and respect for one another grew as we discovered other common interests. We both had spent many a night watching for meteor showers. We both had tagged along with our husbands on extended camping trips and learned to like them. We both lived in all-male families, with three sons each.

As we spent increased time together—team-teaching a class of fourth grade girls, attending conferences for speakers and leaders, planning luncheons—small irritations surfaced. But our friendship remained steady.

Then Selina joined an outspoken political caucus. At first, we discussed the group's issues and aims calmly. As

Selina's convictions intensified, our discourses heated up. She supported one side; I leaned toward the other. One day, her group petitioned our town to recall the city council.

Selina knocked on my door. "You are signing the petition, aren't you?" she asked.

"I'm sorry, Selina; I don't feel that's the way to handle the problem," I answered,

Selina stomped away, and our intimacy withered. I attempted a note or two in hopes of reconciliation but got no reply.

Months later, a mutual friend confided that what had really burned Selina was my refusal to attend a single meeting sponsored by her group where they presented the issues. I had felt unfairly trapped, forced to make an unwanted decision. I paid a great price: the loss of a treasured friend. I couldn't understand why this cause was more important than our friendship. Couldn't we disagree and still remain bosom buddies?

My case is typical of many relationships that break.

Two people are drawn together by mutual attraction or a common tie. Their relationship grows through shared experiences or admiration. The flaws that become evident with closer contact are overcome by a growing bond.

Then, sometimes suddenly, a crisis exposes a new view of the relationship. Formerly unknown opinions or personality traits goad us into unwise words. All the minor irritations of the past combine to feed our minds with rationales for our present actions. A rift results. A once fervid fusion is severed.

Ever since the angel, Lucifer, drew his line in heaven and demanded, "Are you on God's side or mine," all creation has sorrowed over broken relationships.[1]

No matter how hard we try, some relationships will always seem one-sided.

No matter how hard we may try, some relationships will strain and even break.

Relationships are not glossy-smooth "but marred by the ditches and holes into which friends may tumble as they try to stick together."[2]

However, relationships help us glimpse deep mysteries:
• the complex enigmas of human nature
• the hint of spiritual warfare all around us[3]

When these important truths are understood, we begin to realize why every restored relationship is a personal, as well as a spiritual, victory. Every relationship is a school-room experience that tests and develops our character: what kind of stuff are we made of? Who are we, really? What can we do when a relationship dwindles?

Communicate

Candace's parents divorced when she was in junior high. Though the two sides of her parents' families would have little to do with each other after that, Candace tried to keep contact with them all, using care not to antagonize either parent.

At eighteen, Candace decided to marry. Her mother had no objections, but Candace put off telling her father about the engagement. "No daughter of mine is going to be tied down before she's through college," he had often told her. Candace dreaded the lectures and scene she'd have to endure. Meanwhile, she had blurted the news to several cousins on her mother's side.

One evening, her father stopped to visit her and her brother while her mother attended a weekly bridge club. Just as Candace was wondering if this was a good time to mention the approaching wedding, the doorbell rang. Candace opened the door; there stood Aunt Jacque, all smiles.

73

Friends Forever

Aunt Jacque was her mother's sister, disliked by her father, but one of Candace's favorite aunts. She listened in dismay as her aunt exclaimed in a voice that always projected well, "Beth and Susie told me all about the big day. This will be our first wedding in twenty years, you know. Would you like me to fix the flowers?"

Candace mumbled something incoherent.

"Maybe you'd rather I bake the cake or make the gown?"

Candace closed the door as far as she could and still see Aunt Jacque's face. "No! I mean, sure. I mean, I'll talk to you later." She shut the door.

Candace then faced the outburst she had expected from her father. Not only was he agitated about her decision, but he was even more upset that she had held it from him so long, that Aunt Jacque and her family had known about it first. Weeks later, when she and her father finally reconciled, Candace knew she should try to square things with Aunt Jacque. She was so emotionally drained she decided to say nothing and hope Aunt Jacque would take the lead. She finally did—seven years later at a family reunion.

Candace was relieved. "I couldn't bear the silence between us anymore. I didn't want my children to miss out on all the fun we used to have at Aunt Jacque's."

Maintain Integrity

Leah and Kitty had been good friends and neighbors for twenty years. Leah owned and managed a yardage shop; Kitty was a gifted seamstress and artist. When Leah announced one day she planned to sell her store because it was too much for one woman to handle alone, Kitty offered to buy in as a working partner.

After the flurry of legal arrangements, the women spent hours delineating duties and responsibilities. "You keep on taking care of the books and bills," Kitty suggested. "I'll work to drum up more business by offering classes and preparing samples for the store window."

Business boomed. Too well, perhaps. Kitty's classes and outgoing personality made her a hit with all the customers, old as well as new. Leah began to feel she wasn't a vital part of the shop anymore. Kitty began to resent Leah's sullen moods and what she considered unnecessary carping about the neatness of the stock. They had a messy, loud argument that started over nothing: how to sort and file a drawer of patterns.

After two years, the partnership and the friendship soured. Working together had illumined a number of differences in approach that finally ignited an explosion. From the time they dissolved the partnership, no one has heard either of them bad-mouth the other. They made that agreement between themselves, at the advice of a wise lawyer, not only for the sake of the memory of a good friendship, but also in order not to jeopardize future employment opportunities. It's also biblical.

Refuse to Gloat over Misfortunes

A bitter dispute between their husbands on the job separated Nell and Virginia who'd been friends since childhood.

Some time later, the newspaper reported that one of Nell's children had drowned in their pool. Virginia's first fleeting thought was, *Now that no good husband of hers will get what he deserves!* but it was soon replaced with growing sympathy for Nell. She sent Nell and her husband a bouquet and card with the words, "I hurt, too."

Several weeks later Nell visited Virginia. They hugged and wept together. They promised to meet again for lunch once a week, just like they used to.

When the women met for their first reunion, they spoke a few sentences in greeting, then an awkward silence followed. Much had happened before and since their parting. Where should they begin? What could they talk about that wouldn't involve mention of their husbands? How could they keep from opening old wounds? They soon realized this would be a different type of relationship than they'd had before. New rules and sensitivity needed to be observed.

"You come right out and tell me when I need to back off," Nell insisted.

They had some delicate, rocky months, but they now delight in a relationship that's closer than ever. Any restoration process takes conscientious awareness of feelings while the hurts heal.

STEPS TO RESTORING RELATIONSHIPS

When we analyze all our relationships down through the years, we are sure to find some that have hit an impasse. Some may have blown up in our faces; others may still be in reach, but they've regressed to a much cooler level.

Much of the work of relationships has to do with developing a knack of give and take. Like learning to waltz or Texas two-step, we may learn the mechanical steps, yet fine tuning is still needed, the "getting into it" that makes it look graceful and natural. Six steps help us do that:

Initiate Relationships

This is an art, especially with estranged friendships. Remember your common ground. Go back to the beginning and recall the mutual interests that drew you together. Watch for opportunities to approach the person from this common base.

Meanwhile, don't withdraw from other friendships. You need diversity of people to know and love. When a relationship fails, we tend to say, "Never again." To keep all people at arm's length and to avoid the risk of rejection is tempting. Instead, take time to think through your mistakes as well as theirs. Be thankful for all the good things this person brought into your life. With such a positive attitude about your former friend, any new relationship can begin on better footing.

For some people, this is the hardest part: starting a relationship. Their fears, shyness, and insecurity spread a creeping paralysis in social situations. "Shy she was, and I thought her cold," said Alfred Lord Tennyson.

I just returned from a Christmas party of about fifty people held in a huge community hall. I only knew about half the crowd. After a few visits with friends, I spotted a woman whom I didn't know but would like to meet. She had several toddlers scurrying around her, so it was hard to get her attention. Finally, I asked the woman next to me if she knew her. "Oh, sure, she's my next door neighbor."

A perfect in for me. All I had to say was, "Will you introduce me?" I let the moment pass. Why? Because of the old familiar enemy, the gulp and the swallow and the rush of blood to the forehead. I was too self-conscious, too unsure, too shy. All the way home, I scolded myself, *How can a grown woman still have the insecurities of an adolescent?*

If your biggest problem with initiating new or restoring old relationships is due to shyness, I recommend reading *Why Am I Shy?*[4]

Listen Actively

Lazy people rarely maintain lifetime relationships and certainly don't go after the ones that fall by the wayside.

Friends Forever

Do you work at trying to hear what the other person is really saying? Why did your friend act this way? Why did you insist on sticking to your response? Even if you were entirely in the right, how did she react to your hostile attitude?

Is your body and mind giving them full attention? Do you look for tone of voice, level of the eyes, word choices, posture stance, and general appearance for clues to what they're communicating?

When you walk into a room full of people, how much do you notice about individual moods and attitudes? Are you tuned to watch for someone who might be crying out for attention or help or affirmation in a confusion of small talk and banter?

When a relationship splits, the human trend is to ignore that person, to act as if they don't exist, and to emphasize, "Here I am!" rather than, "There you are!" when you enter the same space.

In social situations, lightly talk to your former friend about topics not related to "the problem." This increases the possibility of easing into peaceful exchange later. If your efforts are rebuffed, step back for a time. Don't initiate any more contacts until you receive some kind of welcome sign.

Smooth Relationships

This demands a touch of diplomacy, politics, and compromise. Smoothing also includes tact. Some actions needed in meaningful interchanges aren't rules found in a book or answers sought in a quiz. They're intuitions felt in the heart and soul.

Conflicts of interest, high stakes in a communal property, and other shared concerns need a moderator or one party willing to negotiate. Smoothing includes trying to see the situation from their point of view, stating your side honestly, and being open to learn all you can about the situation.

Smoothing is *not* unloading every one of your thoughts. Discernment knows when you're dumping garbage and when you're dispensing needed, privileged information. In a broken relationship, extra attention needs to be given to looking at the big picture of your care, concern, and commitment, not just what bugs you at the moment.

Another balm for a rough relationship is to ask God for wisdom and intervention. Pray for God's best to happen in his or her life. Ask him to protect your former friend and provide for needs. Prayer can also release your bitterness as you try to reestablish concern. Jesus said an astounding thing, "Love your enemies and pray for those who persecute you" (Matt. 5:44). This is the ultimate smoothing of relationships, at least from your side.

Pray for the people who may be third-party casualties to your breakup. Children, spouses, other friends, and acquaintances can get caught in the cross fire.

Sacrifice

In this busy, hectic world, it would be nice if you could keep your associations buzzing with just a casual, low-key approach. What if you could have a lot of great friends and never have to give up a thing? After all, relationships can be such a bother. They take so much time.

Something would be missing: the cement, the glue that makes a bunch of lone rangers into a community. The most critical sacrificing can happen when you set aside your pride and quietly offer help to someone who has turned on you. Just as traumatic is asking *them* to help *you*.

For how many people would you:

• stop everything and rush to their side

Friends Forever

- donate blood
- invite to come live with you indefinitely
- clean out your savings
- nurse to health
- guardian their children
- give your life
- cover their son's paper route
- make homemade tamales
- telephone long distance once a week
- provide bail

The most dramatic example of sacrificing for someone who's broken all contact is God's sending Jesus to a planet of alienated creatures to show them he still loves, still cares, and still wants to provide a way to reestablish contact.

Pace Relationships

Are you trying too hard? Moving too fast? Around too much? Do you give space to breathe, room to think, freedom to walk away?

The right pacing may be accomplished only through a process of trial and error. To clutch too tightly can bring death to a relationship and prevent it from stirring to life again.

The Bible warns, "Let your foot rarely be in your neighbor's house, Lest he become weary of you" (Prov. 25:17 NASB).

Present your case to your friend. Assure him or her of your care and desire to make things right. Then let them choose.

If the situation keeps gnawing at you and stunting your effectiveness in daily responsibilities, find an objective, mature listener to whom you can spill out your story. Then, do some self-listening—to your own words and emotions and to the feedback you're given.

Attend to Detail

Do you make people feel important when you greet them or when they depart? Do they receive more than a nonchalant "yeah?" when they call by phone? Do you pay attention to the dates, people, places, and interests that are important to them? Details like this provide the seasoning to otherwise humdrum exchanges.

Watch for opportunities to show kindness. Practice inward integrity by greeting your former friend with a smile when you pass and immediately remind yourself of their good points. If he or she suffers an accident or wins a promotion, send a card. These tiny tokens are sometimes the only doors open to you.

Even with careful consideration to these six steps, there will still be the heartache of love won and lost. But none of the effort is a waste. Treasure is still among the rubble. What do we gain by striving for affection that lasts for decades and receive instead an overnight express rejection?

You receive a clear, honest view of the potential uncertainties and disappointments of life.

You face head-on a meaty challenge that helps keep you humble and compassionate for others who grieve.

You've been given a chance to prove you can suffer one of life's most devastating sorrows and survive.

You can evaluate the relationships that remain and treasure them even more by implementing the lessons you've learned.

Love is a decision of the will.

Anyone, at any time, for any reason, can choose to dam up their affections toward you. This closing of the heart and spirit can blind them. Suddenly, they see you one-dimensional. You can't please them, no matter what you do.

Friends Forever

You can count on only two relationships:
* *Friendship with God*
* *Friendship with any man or woman who determines they will stick with you, no matter what.*

TIME TO CONSIDER

1. Read Genesis 13. What is happening in the relationship between Abraham and Lot?

2. The following letter was sent to counselors who write an advice column for a magazine. How would you answer the woman?

"After friends stayed with me recently, I received a letter from the wife telling me that I had said things that hurt her feelings. I responded immediately with a sincere apology, although I couldn't recall some of the things she mentioned. She wrote back with another list of injuries, some of which went back fifteen years. I asked her forgiveness and tried to rectify what I could, even though I wasn't aware of the situations she was recalling. What else can I do?"[5]

3. Describe an incident you have observed (or heard about) in which people restored a broken relationship. How did they do it?

4. Are there ever times when a relationship is best left in its broken state? Describe such a situation.

5. Do you have a relationship that you regret isn't as close as it used to be? What could you do to begin to initiate restoration? When?

7
...
The Long Road Home–and Back Again

Rose silk legs swish softly
. . . home
up battered steps
peeled gray by midwest storms

A hesitant knock

Gingham and calico charms
the startled brows
as seasoned arms fling back
the long, lost years

Up in the attic
an ancient treasure box
. . . lies open

crippled dolls and tattered linens
sprawl like angel wings
to stir the peach scented cedar

She scoops a hugful
wheels them back in Samsonite
to tuck them high
   on the fourteenth floor[1]

Mom and Dad.

Whatever you call them, whoever claims those roles may hold the key to your ability to generate and maintain a wide circle of lifetime relationships. If so, the most important task in your present is making peace with your past.

If the past was painful, the wound must be cared for.

If the past was wonderful, much better than now, the pleasure must be applied to softly spice, not distort, the present.

Dad and Mom.

They can be your most complex, and most certain, lifetime relationships.

Above all the other relationships we're privileged to navigate, this is one that we must always honor and learn how to leave.

HOW TO RELINQUISH YOUR PARENTS

"For this reason a man will leave his father and mother: (Gen. 2:24; Matt. 19:5).

"We think we need to have . . . perfect parents and so on to meet our deepest needs. . . . Many of us try to use people to give us quality life, hoping they will bring us lasting fulfillment."[2] Admitting and changing our self-centered approach to relationships takes courage, honesty, and the willingness to take on a life-long homework assignment.

Right dealings with your parents (and siblings) can establish the core example for all your other relationships: how you treat older men as fathers; younger men as brothers; older women as mothers; and younger women as sisters.[3]

Whether or not your relationship up to now has been satisfactory, it's never too late to leave your parents. *Shift* is needed in this relationship. No longer, "How are they taking care of me?" but "How am I treating them?" Can you remember a time when you gave your parents a healthy, wholesome, peaceful release?

Parents need their freedom—freedom to be imperfect, freedom to make mistakes, freedom to care for themselves, freedom to be forgiven, freedom to dream their own dreams that may or may not include you or your family.

The process of leaving parents can cause almost unbearable tensions.

Let Them Go

You can no longer depend on your parents for your financial, emotional, and social well-being. How sad to see adult children who have all their social contacts tied up with their parents. When they are separated by a move or death, they can become lonely, with no built-up resources for making friends. Other subtle dependencies exist, too.

"Dad really shocked me," Breanne spilled out one day. "Not only that, he let me down. We always had good times together. Even after I married, we had lunch alone several times a month. After Mom died, I cared for his every need. I helped him pay the bills, buy the groceries, and make his appointments—just like Mom did. Now, a year later, he's married again."

"Doesn't that take some of the pressure off you?" I suggested.

"No! It's worse. Emma, his new wife, has never had children and announced on their wedding day, 'Please don't call me Mom or have the kids call me Grandma. I'm just not the type. And please call before you visit. I don't enjoy surprises.' " Breanne dabbed the new rush of tears with a tissue.

"You have adjustments to make, but at least you don't have to pretend with this woman," I offered.

"You don't understand. Not only have I lost a mother, but now I've lost my dad as well. He's gone—the dad I once knew, the camaraderie we shared. She's stolen him from me."

Adult children face similar emotions—anger, fear, disbelief, loneliness, guilt, doubts, and feelings of abandonment—when their parents divorce after umpteen years of marriage. Suddenly, the family breaks up into jealous units. The model of fidelity for your own marriage disappears. A sense of helplessness that problems can *never* be worked out grows. Your heart is torn into two warring factions—love and identification with father, love and identification with mother. Life is complicated by having to put these two now separate lives together in your thinking while being caught in their battle. You often have to choose sides or play one against the other in order to keep peace. You have to learn how to trust others again. Letting go becomes essential in giving your parents and you space to work out the new family arrangements.[4]

Give Them Up

Give up your expectations of them. Give up allowing them to control your decisions, give up constantly asking their advice. Be willing to make your own mistakes, without blaming your parents. Practice saying, "I decided this. I choose to do that. I accept the consequences."

Darcy is the mother of twin girls, now eight years old. "When the girls were toddlers, I found myself favoring one of them. One always pleased me; the other made me angry at least once a day. I couldn't understand why until I talked to my mother one day. Something she said about my sister brought back a rush of memories.

"I never knew my dad. He left us when I was two. I always wanted my mom's attention and love, but all my attempts just irritated her. She showered her love on my sister instead. Now, I was taking out my resentment on one of the twins. For me to realize this was healing. I determined to change. I purposely paid individual care to each of my girls, especially the one who had experienced my wrath. I felt I was remaking the past, giving myself the love I had so dearly wanted. I also had a glimpse into why Mom couldn't show me the love I now realize had always been there. My stubborn ways, so much like her own, closed her up emotionally. She didn't have the buffer of Dad's love to help her open up to me."

The social task of learning to initiate and form relationships begins when you're a child. Through your childhood friendships, you learn to think through the consequences of your behavior and to weigh the relative merits of possible outcomes.

"Those whose parents are unhappily married try to avoid conflict when they play with their friends," says John Gottman, a developmental psychologist at the University of Washington in Seattle. He's been studying young children from different family backgrounds interacting with other children. "They don't seem to learn how to manage conflict with their friends very well. They also don't show the same joy and excitement about friendships that other kids have."[5]

Similar research conducted at Duke University showed a strong relationship between parents' skills at making friends and the child's skills. These experiences can carry over into adolescence and adulthood.

No parent is perfect.

You can't continue to blame your parents for your reaction to supposed slights or grievous wrongs. As an adult, you must deal with *your responses* to their actions. Learning how to forgive and release a father or mother can be a vital turning point in healing a handicapped personality.

To honorably let them go and give them up is possible.

HOW TO HONOR YOUR PARENTS

"Honor your father and your mother, so that you may live long in the land" (Ex. 20:12).

Receive the Love They Offer

Gather up whatever bits or bushels full of love they send your way and collect them as reserves for the conflicts and misunderstandings.

Think through how your parent communicates love. Through the hint of subtle words? Through hugs? Through a surprising gift? Through a phone call for no reason at all? Through a fumbling apology? Through long, newsy letters? Through a rare note of appreciation? Through a homecooked meal?

Find out how *their* parents showed *them* love. Does this have any affect on their display of affection to you?

Every family unit is a culture all its own. A distinct language is learned, with certain words having special meanings. There are rituals: "We always do things this way." There's a history, a family lore of memories and experiences. Within this cultural experience, love is shared if you can decipher the code. Often, the way we express (or can't express) love to other people is a learned ability growing out of our family culture.[6]

Adulthood arrives in these small sudden exchanges more than in well-heralded major crises. And the final moment of assuming adulthood may be when we inherit the legacy, become the keeper of traditions, the curator of our family's past and future memories. When the holidays are at *our* houses. The reunions at *our* instigation. When the traditions are carried on, or cast aside, because of choices that we make. . . . Only once it's refused, it disappears.[7]

Give Them What Love You Can

Unconditional love is the highest human ability possible. It's love like God loves.

It's love no matter what others look like, no matter what their assets, liabilities, handicaps. No matter what we expect them to be, no matter how they act—even when at times we may detest their behavior.

Listen to your parents like an attentive daughter. Refuse to gripe about them to your family and friends. Provide for their physical needs, if it's within your ability. Keep attuned to the thinking of their generation.

If you have children of your own, allow the grandparents to forge their own relationships with them, to have an open road to become permanent friends.

Accept the family order—how you assess that each parent treats you in comparison with your siblings—with grace.

Try to appreciate their tastes in music.

Friends Forever

Try to show empathy with their concerns, with that which troubles them and they consider important.

If needed, and as far as is possible for you, help them live out the remainder of their years free from poverty, untended sickness, or abject loneliness.

Show them love in the way they understand best.

Betsy lives on Long Island, four hundred miles from her mom. "Once a year, on one of my long weekend vacations, I fly to my hometown and spend the whole time baking and sewing and taking care packages to Mom's neighbors and friends. That's the way she shows love. That's the way she receives love, by my entering into her world and her activities. It took me a lot of years to figure this out. Once I did, our relationship improved immensely."

Persist

No matter how old you or they are, keep building your relationship. Don't let your parental bond fall into a rut, or worse, into a bitter fallout.

"So many things are wrong with my family, I don't know where to begin," Yongsue complains. "Both my parents have been married and divorced twice. I don't know how long their present mates will last. My children hardly know them. Grandma's always off on some trip. Grandpa never comes to see them or calls them on the phone.

"The whole thing really hit me last summer. Not one of them came to my daughter's wedding. Not one. They treated it so casually, like 'What's the big deal?' If it weren't for my trust and faith in God, I'd completely cut them out of my life.

"But my husband made me prepare photo albums of pictures from the wedding and take one to each parent. I couldn't believe how much they appreciated it. My father even blurted out that he was sorry he didn't go. 'I just never feel comfortable in church,' he told me. I'm starting to understand, and I'll keep trying."

To honor means to:
- give value by paying a price
- esteem as precious
- treat as equals or better
- respect (attitude) and protect (action)
- genuinely care
- invest the best you have to give
- recognize a debt to your heritage
- encourage rather than criticize

To dishonor means to:
- shame what they have produced or achieved
- constantly remind of past wrongs
- allow guilt to build up defenses

HOW TO LOVE A PRODIGAL PARENT

Some parents have purposely removed themselves from your family circle, and they are difficult to honor.

Some refuse to accept you for who you are.

Some have lifestyles that embarrass.

Some insist on habitual harangues that alienate.

To show a measure of honor is still possible.

1. *Do the things you would like to do if the situation were better*. "If Dad appreciated my efforts, I'd feel differently," you might say. That's an excuse for not doing anything. If it's the right thing to do, do it.

2. *Show their peer group that you honor them*. You might live a different lifestyle, but could you occasionally step out of your mold to demonstrate respect? Honor your parents on their terms.

How are their friends honored by their families? That might be a clue to how you can show them the same honor. If they're honored in a way their friends notice, they will most likely feel flattered and appreciated, even if they don't tell you.

3. *Consistently show honor.* If you've invited them for dinner for the last four years and they've refused every time, keep right on asking. By your actions, remind them they can withdraw from you but they are not forgotten by you.

4. *Consider the long-term investment.* Don't look for easy rewards or instant changes. You're working through complicated sessions in complex relationships. It may take a lifetime, or more, to see the results.

5. *Ask God's help.* You might not have a praying parent. You might not be accustomed to praying about something so natural, so ordinary, as misunderstandings with parents. The Creator of families knows how to untangle the messes and is willing to show you the best next step. Find a Christian friend to pray with you about your situation.[8]

Mary is thirty-two years old. At age sixteen, she moved out on her own. At twenty-two, she moved twelve hundred miles from home and didn't communicate with her mother for ten years. She had just reestablished her maternal relationship when her mom discovered she had lung cancer. In a matter of weeks, Mary's mother died.

"It's not fair!" Mary wails. "I was just starting to realize I had a mother; now she's gone!"

Mary can mourn the future she won't have, but she is responsible for the past she forfeited.

"How fragile is this sinew of generations. How tenuous the ceremonial ties that hold families together . . . while they change as imperceptibly and inevitably as cells change in a single human body."[9]

A parent can only last for a lifetime.

TIME TO CONSIDER

1. How has your relationship with your parent(s) helped or hindered your ability to make and keep good relationships?

2. Is it easy or difficult for you to honor your parent(s)? Why?

3. Have you completely "left" your parent(s) yet? If not, in what ways?

4. For what are you most grateful to your parents(s)?

5. A woman I know was physically and verbally abused as a child by her father. She required extensive counseling after she came to Christ to become the person she wanted to be. Just when she believed she was making strong progress, her father suffered a stroke. After agonizing deliberations, she decided to take her father into her home so she could nurse him back to health. It was a wrenching, yet healing, experience for both of them.

If you had to face a situation like this, what resources would you call upon to endure the daily emotional struggles?

8

...

The Ultimate, Permanent Invasion of Privacy

They don't make men like they used to.

Anyway, the statistics give that impression.

A man and his woman.

A woman and her man.

They just don't last a lifetime anymore.

Marriage and divorce. The only things that still go hand in hand.

To love a man for life. Can it still be done?

My husband and I both said, "I do," before we knew we didn't. We didn't match up in our expectations, in approaches to communication, in what we wanted in life, and in our personality makeup.

Years later, on one of our camping trips, we answered one of those intensive questionnaires that many engaged couples complete in premarital counseling. For several days in the Cascades in northern California, we listened, discussed, argued, and finally rejoiced. A glimmer of light dawned. We finally understood why our relationship took so much constant, tender, watchful care.

I believe we are typical of most couples. We forget there's always more to learn. So many spouses give up right before the good part.

Based on Hippocrates' ancient formula, we discovered that I'm a melancholy and Steve's a choleric personality. One counselor told us, "Cholerics are rarely attracted to melancholies. When they are, they're incompatible."

We took some more tests. One revealed Steve to be a dominant "D" type. I tipped the graph as a compliant "C."

Aha, I thought, *That should make an excellent team: one chief and one Indian.*

Not true. According to studies of behavioral patterns, a "D" combined with a "C" constitutes a poor pairing for cooperation and accomplishing tasks. The "D" wants action; the "C" needs time to analyze and think. Both vie for control and power, but each in his or her own way.

Another more finite testing system confirmed our atypical choice in mating. This identified our particular individual blends as almost nonexistent. My personality type comprises one percent of the total human population; Steve's breed makes up five percent. The odds that we'd even find each other were pretty slim. Yet we sat next to each other all four years of high school English.

Our relationship is more than what fits the curve of the charts. We've enjoyed a long, happy marriage that's into its second quarter of a century. We've also worked through the stress and tears of close teamwork as writing partners. We know what it means to work through the maze of incompatibility.

I have to be honest with you. Little progress was made until we both called on God for his help. He took us through the painful steps of taming our bulldog egos so we could find a measure of true love. A love that sees the worst but encourages the best. A love that's weathered so many upheavals, the next one's taken in stride. A love that warms up with just a word or a look. A love that sizzles. A love that makes individual differences complement rather than divide.[1]

That's why I feel a spark of empathy and understanding when I hear someone say: "I think I married the wrong person."

I want to tell them: "Hey, don't give up. Your relationship can turn out to be one of the best kinds. If you're willing to try. If you're willing to stick in there. If you're willing to make him your lifetime friend."

You don't have to know everything about *marriage* to make a good one. You only have to figure out how to live in peace and productivity with *this one man*. That comes with daily personal experience over a long season of getting to know each other. Books like this can offer tips that provide possible shortcuts.

SHORTCUTS THAT WORKED FOR ME
Remember to Tell Him You're Sorry

No couple has plumbed the width and depth of all they are, all that could be, and all that motivates their thoughts and actions. That's why it's imperative to spend lots of time talking. Moods and circumstances often change abruptly. It can be a full-time job to prod yourself to communicate, to listen with both the eyes and the mind, and to realize when to keep quiet.

Richard and Mary Strauss tell of their "love fights." They seek solutions to conflicts that will *increase* their love for one another, rather than merely trying to win. They believe the best way to resolve conflict is to seek a solution that will satisfy the needs of both partners. They ask themselves, "What valuable new thing can I learn from this that will help me be a better person?" "What is my spouse really feeling right now?" "How would he like me to respond?"[2]

Learning how to talk to your husband could be the challenge of a lifetime. The trick is to "become a confidante, rather than a sparring partner."[3] You must articulate your needs and desires and find creative responses to anger-producing situations. Think before you spout.

When something bothers me, I go underground. I submerge the irritation until it festers into a gory wound. I mull over the problem and become consumed by it before I give any clue as to what's going on.

By his example, Steve has taught me to speak out on an issue, loud and clear, in a rational and logical way. He forces me to consider the results if I don't plod through the problem but hope it will go away. A method that has greatly helped me is to write in simple outline form exactly what is bugging me before I confront him. This helps me calm down, think straight, and get right to the point.

One day, Steve explained that he didn't like the way I changed a final draft on one of his stories. "You smoothed it out too much. It didn't sound like rough old me. Those were your expressions, not mine," he said.

"Well," I retorted. "You can type all your own finals from now on! That way they'll really sound like you."

Later, I cooled down. I even considered an apology. The temptation crossed my mind to ignore the whole scene. *After all*, I reasoned, *Steve's not a brooder. He'll soon forget it.* I could take him for granted and allow the gritty sand of pride to wear away our trust.

However, I did recant, and we discussed several alternatives to help us correct and rewrite with more integrity in the future. What if I hadn't? That one stubborn choice of my will could have built a wedge of habits between us.

Isn't that the way most relationships break down? A secret, private resolve is made that short-circuits the ability to restore free, open harmony. Hurt feelings are closer to the surface next time.

"It is a whole bunch of really *little* things that can ruin a marriage, because that is what our wills tend to be made up of: petty, selfish desires. Only another person can challenge and confront us at this deep personal level of our own private will and reveal to us how petty it is. Only a real encounter with another real person, day in and day out, can begin to prick the bubble of the ego."[4]

Dr. Gary Chapman tells of advice that was given to him and his bride-to-be by the minister. "When you are angry, take turns talking." He explained that each should be given three to five minutes to state his or her understanding of the issue. Without interruption. Without mentally rehearsing their rebuttal blast.[5]

Join His Adventures

My husband's a wanderer, a restless pioneer who should've been born in the eighteen-hundreds, when the West begged for explorers. During the first twenty years of marriage, we moved nineteen times. The longest space I had called home provided three consecutive Christmases.

Many of those moves, I went kicking and screaming. Then I'd discover new friends and vital experiences worth the uprooting after all. Now that I know there's life beyond the safe and secure ruts, I don't panic when I hear the familiar preamble, "I've been thinking about something, Jan. . . ."

Steve has also learned to respect my feelings and thoughts. If I ever said, "Absolutely not!" he'd stay. He considers what places there'll be for me and the children in his new frontier.

Steve sees life as a mountain to be conquered. I peer at it through a dark tunnel that requires extensive indoor lighting. I'm learning to tolerate (even enjoy) his mountain; he takes occasional, educational peeks into my tunnel.

Fight the tranquilizing effect of creeping boredom in a marriage. Find new adventures. Together.

Realize You're In Training

"Marriage is a lifelong unraveling of that person page by page."[6]

Not everyone gets it right the first year or the fifth or even last week. We're all learners. That's the fun; that's the frustration.

"Marriages are a lot like a pair of glasses. We live in them every day and often take them for granted. We bend them, stretch them, carelessly stack a dozen things on top of them, and sometimes leave them lying around forgotten."[7]

Lifetime relationships must be . . .

nourished
stimulated
cherished
cultivated
fed
sustained
and nurtured

. . . with nutrients necessary for their life and growth.

That sums up the creative energy and emphasis required to work through incompatibility. Many marriages die in midlife due to simple neglect.

Sometimes every ounce of adrenaline needs to flow to give me control, to contend with my belligerence, my knee-jerk defensiveness, my compulsion to justify everything I've ever done. Each year gets easier as I keep practicing.

This scene used to get a lot of replay.

"Jan, it's 8:00."

"Uh huh."

"Isn't Aaron supposed to be getting ready for bed?"

"Yep, I told him."

"The bath water's not running."

"Nooo . . ."

"Why don't you run up there and take care of him?"

Silence.

Long sigh. "Well, *somebody's* got to be sure he's not late again. You know how grouchy he is in the mornings." Mad dash upstairs with a martyred look in my direction.

More silence from me, this time poignant with anger.

This thorn of misunderstanding was finally removed when we talked it through, calmly, one winter evening several years ago.

Steve's main concern was that Aaron got to bed exactly on time. I wanted Aaron to learn to be told a thing just once and learn the discipline of meeting a time deadline without my nagging and hovering. I interpreted Steve's conversation as a criticism of my mothering and cause for some well-planned retort.

One of the most difficult statements I have ever learned to say is, "Thanks for helping me to see that." The words can grate in my brain, clutch at my throat, burn in my stomach. But they're not impossible. They may not be the first words I say; but more and more, they are the second. That simple statement eases many a choleric/melancholic clash.

Friends Forever

We all have negative emotions that must be managed.

There's no way around it. Two people shuffling in and out of the same bathroom and floundering around in the same bed have got to be adaptable and flexible or soon stiffen into strangers who silently pass in the night.

"We must understand love; we must be able to teach it, to create it, to predict it, or else the world is lost to hostility and to suspicion."[8]

Don't Expect Him to Fulfill Every Need

No human can do that. Certainly not the imperfect man you married. He has wounds and hurts of his own to overcome. He has ambitions of his own to reach. He, too, may have a lot to learn about lifetime loving.

A balance of outside interests and friends can provide needed space and release from assuming that this man must make you happy, healed, and whole in every way. We must understand we may have unconscious expectations—"primarily that our partner will love us the way our parents never did. We expect our partner to do it all—satisfy our unmet childhood needs, complement lost parts of ourselves, nurture us in a consistent and loving way, and be eternally available to us."[9]

Be His Best Friend

Value *his* needs by directing more of your thoughts and energies to meeting those needs.

When I wanted to explore writing, Steve scooted me out the door to a writers' seminar. When I recognized his writing potential, I nudged him to join me.

When the pressures of responsibility drag him down, I encourage him to get away for a few days by himself. He'll camp in the mountains, explore ghost towns, or backpack in the wilderness.

Then he'll care for our youngest son so I can slip off to the lake for a day of reading or contemplation. Or he'll arrange finances so I can attend a conference or join a club.

Amid the piles of dirty-dish dregs of romance and garbage-pail realities, you must have the drive to encourage your mate and develop the continuing desire for intimacy.

Steve's idea of perfect entertainment is horseback riding, rodeos, and Merle Haggard concerts. I'd rather listen to the New York Symphony Orchestra, watch an old classic romance movie, or read a George McDonald novel. But we've discovered we agree on Kenny Rogers and The Judds concerts. I've even added a few pioneer stories to my personal library.

Keep Sex Alive

Women who work at their commitment to make marriage last often discover a startling truth. Sex improves with age. Sex seasons with practice. When explored with one man in the relaxing, satisfying atmosphere of loyalty and trust.

God provided this balm to ease the bristles of bumping up against the faults and frailties of another human day in and day out. Used right, in marriage, it's a boon to a lifetime commitment. Outside of marriage, it's a bomb.

"I'd give anything to do it all over differently," Corrine confides. "I lost three of the best friends I ever had. My husband. Donna. Her husband, Geoff. All because I couldn't control my sexual curiosity, my appetite for feeling another man's arms. I miss Donna and her fun ways. I miss the long talks Geoff and I had over the fence. And how I miss my husband! I really loved him. We had a good marriage. Why did I let it happen?"

TO LOVE, ADD THESE FOUR ...

Feelings of romantic attraction come and go. Any old twosome thrown together on the strength of sex appeal alone can endure several years of coupling. Those who want to last the duration—those who dare to say as Robert Browning did, "Grow old along with me! The best is yet to be. The last of life, for which the first was made"—will want to add more. They will thrive on the challenge to see it to the end. Those brave visionaries will broaden their definition of love to include:

contentment
courtesy
courage
creativity

The most important attitude you can have toward your husband is *contentment,* a renewed satisfaction, after all the warts and blemishes have been exposed, to have chosen this man, above all others, as your life's partner.

No more unfavorable comparisons. No more trying to completely overhaul him. Just relishing the pure joy of who he is, not who he is not. Make peace with your selection.

The highest grace you can bestow on your mate is *courtesy,* the public respect and private attentiveness to his opinions, ideas, and dreams. Remembering the "please's" and "thank you's" and "how are you really today's?"

As you face disappointments and disillusionments, the utmost sacred gift you can incorporate into the mood of your marriage is *courage,* that word of hope, that action of help, that willingness to try once more, to see what another day will bring.

Facing the bills another month. Encouraging him in his job. Praising his attempts at fathering. Telling him what you appreciate about his lovemaking. Understanding his struggles to communicate.

Finally, the best of yourself you can invest in this chief plum of relationships is *creativity*. The same passion and energy and ingenuity you would give to a dream job, you measure out right in your home.

Kidnap him from work for a big overnighter at a nearby resort. Purchase a new nightie *he* will like. Read chapters from books he never has time for when you're traveling. Once a week, put extra effort into a meal: placemats, centerpiece, a favorite dessert, a new sauce for the vegetables, and a chunk of meat the way he likes it. Prepare a thorough report on how you can save money, purchase that boat he wants, and prepare for the kids' college, even if that raise doesn't come through.

Every marriage feels the pinch of confinement at times. Every couple must face and cope with a multitude of crises. Through these tests of endurance, you can prove the fabric of your relationship.

That's why marriage is meant for life.

It takes that long to explore all the potential pleasures. It takes that long to plumb the depths of the potent bliss.

LIFE AFTER DIVORCE

Sometimes you have no choice. Other times, you do. In either case, some of you have already made The Big Escape. You thought.

Divorce ends it all. Doesn't it? No more having to get along. No more complications. No more problems. No stresses. No more having to deal with the whole thing. Right?

Wrong.

A former husband is still a lifetime relationship. The marriage bond is such an intricate intertwining that a complete severing of the influence and confrontation that it infuses into your life cycle isn't possible.

Here's how two women kept the relationship going in the right direction.

An ex-wife wrote to Dear Abby, the advice columnist, with the message: "Forgiveness is a gift to the giver. I speak from personal experience."

She had taken legal action against her ex-husband for payment of back child support. At the last minute, she withdrew the court action for the sake of her sons, who had always had a good relationship with their drinking father. She feared this would alienate them from each other. "As it turned out, that was the wisest decision I ever made. Seven years later Rob was dead, at age 48. I'm glad I let Rob off the hook. We kept a cordial relationship, and I'm not plagued with guilt."[10]

The other case has to do with an acquaintance of ours. Her husband dumped her for another woman. Suzanne suffered with bitterness and anger for several years. Then she realized how much she was making her three daughters suffer.

"I decided since I couldn't change the situation, I'd change me. I got a job I liked, stopped denouncing Jim and his new wife, and got my attention on other pursuits. I couldn't believe all I began to learn about myself. I could *survive!* I could be likable. I made lots of new friends, both male and female, and felt free and alive for the first time since he left me. Now I can talk to Jim about the girls without my stomach screwing up in knots, and the girls are more at peace."

Marriage.

Once you've entered the inner sanctum, that private domain, you're never the same again.

Every nerve seems jangled, every dream appears snarled,

until that amazing day you settle the issue once and for all.

You and this man are in the fray—for better or worse—for life.

TIME TO CONSIDER

1. What are ten things you want in the man who will be your best friend? Show this list to your husband and ask his comments. Invite him to make his own list.

a.   f.

b.   g.

c.   h.

d.   i.

e.   j.

2. You receive a letter in the mail announcing the most unbelievably good news you could imagine. Who will you want to tell first? Second? Why?

3. Describe a couple who seem to you to be the best of friends. What clues do you look for?

4. A friend, Susan Clonts, presently of Lake Jackson, Texas, critiqued parts of this book for me while I was completing it. She remarked, "It's hard enough to develop a relationship between two people, but much more difficult when you include a group of four or more. It's important to find a few couples that both you and your spouse are close to. It seems that my generation, early thirties, does not have the strong 'couple-friends' our parents had. I can think of some reasons—mobility, two-income families, less time outdoors due to air conditioning, TV, etc.—but I really would like advice on how to develop these friendships."

What thoughts do you have on this subject?

5. What is the most important thing an engaged couple could do to improve the prospects for their future marriage?

9
...
A Little Child Will Lead Them

Not every woman will bear a child of her own.

But every woman needs a child in her circle of lifetime relationships. A child she can watch grow. A child who can know that, whatever happens, someone really cares. A child to touch her heart, break her will, and keep her human.

What if the world had no children? Just adults. Always, ever, and only. What would be taken from us?

For one thing, nostalgia. No "they lived happily ever after." No "once upon a time" moments.

Children are a gift of God. They can ease the pain of a lost love. They can provide hope of a better future. They are symbolic of all that pleases God.[1]

There'd be fewer warnings of the urgency of the passing of time. Fewer reminders of the fun things of life: olives on fingers, bubbles, Disneyland, cotton candy, and swings.

Children provide impetus for getting involved in life, crusading for causes affecting today's people, as well as future generations. They prompt us to care.

They see ordinary, mundane scenes in new ways.

Who would keep your mind active by asking "a thousand questions that the wisest man cannot answer"?[2]

Who would keep your heart alive and beating by tugs and pulls and views into what life's really all about?

Who would remind you of the growth, the development, the steady pattern of life, the hope that comes from birth and new beginnings?

Who would make you laugh? cry? sing?

Who else could possibly keep you humble?

Who but a child?

"Every child born into the world is a new thought of God, an ever-fresh and radiant possibility."[3]

There's no danger of our suddenly developing a childless world. The earth's crammed with them. However, many children may lose their most precious gift: their childhood.

Childhood is no longer what the late child psychologist Selma Fraiberg called "The Magic Years." The magic's been replaced with adult clutter and traumas—violence, stress, competition, insecurity, pressure to succeed, abuse, drugs, peer pressure, family instability, the push to grow up faster, values that exalt self-centeredness, winning at all costs, the accumulation of things, adult-life decisions and responsibilities, and a media awareness that brings today's worldwide crises into the living room.

Daily, thousands of children are added to the list: *Missing: Could It Happen to Your Child?*

An estimated thirteen hundred stepfamilies are formed each day.

Each year, an estimated 1.2 million children are battered by an adult, usually a parent or relative.

By the time he or she has reached eighteen, the average American child has watched eighteen thousand murders on TV.

The rate of suicide for those under fifteen has tripled, while all other age groups have decreased.

Dial-a-porn records a child's voice inviting sexual contact. R- and X-rated videos are now played in the family living room.

By ninth grade, one child in six has tried marijuana; one in three has tried alcohol.[4]

Pressure to learn is stepped up as higher curricula is introduced into lower grades.

Costly brand-name clothes and toys are lavished on them, yet fewer kids seem "basically happy."[5]

You need kids. At least one.

They also need you.

WHAT YOU CAN MEAN TO A CHILD

Not every child will have faithful, loving parents; but every child desperately needs at least one consistent, caring adult to see them through the pangs of growing up. You can:

Provide a Place of Refuge

"In the man whose childhood has known caresses and kindness, there is always a fibre of memory that can be touched to gentle issues."[6]

Kim loved her job but hated her apartment. All she could afford was a fourth floor flat, just underneath a family that seemed to be growing, literally, by leaps and bounds. Her only moments of quiet came between two and five o-clock in the morning, when the little darlings zonked.

Friends Forever

On occasion, she'd see them in the hall, at least three wiry bodies zooming around a tired-looking mom. The Gonzalez family, she heard.

One evening about ten, Kim couldn't take it any longer. She ran up the stairs and knocked on the door. A small brown face peered through. "You've got to stop that noise!" she blurted out to the startled boy. "I can't think, I can't relax, I can't sleep!"

The boy burst into tears. "We can't help it! We get so scared! We try, but we hear scary noises."

"Where's your mom?"

"I don't know. I think she's with Fred."

Kim gazed around the dingy, ramshackle room. Two other heads stared from behind a couch. A diapered toddler crept along a far wall. Kim left a note for the mother and led the children down stairs. She fed them, bathed them, read them a story, then tucked them into two sleeping bags on the floor. "I'll leave this light on, but no noise."

They were all asleep before she got into bed.

By six, when Kim's alarm rang, the children's mother still hadn't come to get them. Kim found her upstairs with a man. His name wasn't Fred. "How sweet of you," she slurred. "I figured they were all right. You can do that anytime you want."

"You can't leave them alone like that!" Kim said, still in shock.

"You aren't going to report me," the woman hissed, suddenly sober and hostile.

"I . . . I don't know. But those kids could get hurt."

Within a few days, the woman moved out. Kim found this scrawled note tacked to her door. "Lady Kim, that was the funnest nite we ever had!" Four illegible names sprawled at the bottom. Kim cried and ran to the landlady to try to find where they went. But she never saw the children again.

"Be sure to rent floor five to a family with kids," she told the landlady.

Pass on Your Knowledge and Experiences

"Those who educate children well are more to be honored than those who produce them; for these only gave them life, those the art of living well."[7]

For years, Corrie ten Boom, her sister, Betsy (both of whom never married), and her father housed foster children, mostly teenagers, in their narrow, three-story stucco and brick watchshop in Haarlem, Holland, called the Beje. A visitor commented one time to Corrie's father that he was astonished at the noise and laughter in their house. Her father said, "Our children are such good kids . . . why they never quarrel and are always ready to help each other. They're just angels."

Meanwhile, Corrie sighed and went upstairs to talk to one of the girls, Puck, who had been sent to her room for the "angelic" way she had said, "I hate Lessie!"

As Puck sat in the corner of her bed, curled up in that defiant position children take when they know they're going to be punished, Corrie said, "Puck, don't you know that Jesus says hatred is murder in God's eyes? He told us we must love our enemies."

"Well, I can't love Lessie!" A trace of tears rose in her eyes. "What must I do, Tante Kees [the kids' name for Corrie]? Such hateful thoughts come in my heart."

"John says, 'If we confess our sins, he is faithful and just to forgive us our sins, and to cleanse us from all unrighteousness' (1 John 1:9 KJV). Shall we go to Him now and tell Him everything?"

Puck and Lessie became the greatest of friends. Years later, during World War II, Puck was in a Japanese concentration camp in Indonesia.

Puck told Corrie after the war, "When I was beaten, I thought of you and Tante Betsie and Opa and remembered what you had taught me about love for my enemies." The teaching had lasted through even this trial.[8]

Provide a Role Model

An old Scotsman, Captain Grose, wisely said, in his own peculiar way, "A chield's amang you takin' notes, And faith he'll prent it."[9]

You could become quite a memorable individual to some child. You could be a person who enriches their store of knowledge of human nature. You could be the someone who encourages them in their future enterprises or challenges.

An author was interviewed by a TV host recently. "Where do you find your stories and characters?" she said. "They're so distinctive, so compelling."

The man laughed. "Most of them come from my neighborhood growing up in St. Louis. And mainly, all my heroines are a variation of Mrs. Findley, one of the most interesting, exciting people I've ever known. She made root beer sodas every afternoon for all us kids, and the yarns she would spin. . . ."

A child can also help you assess your lifestyle. Do you set a good example? What causes you shame under close inspection?

You Can Stand in the Gap, Help Ease Sorrows and Upsets

Leo Buscaglia noticed the girl in the sea of faces on his first day of teaching. Nervous, he latched onto her animated face. Her smile gave him strength to go on. When he'd say something, she'd nod and write it down. She made Leo feel she cared about what he was so awkwardly trying to say.

Leo asked all his students to visit his office sometime during the semester. He waited with special interest for this one girl, Liani, so he could tell her how she had pulled him through that class. She never came. When she missed two weeks of class, he checked with the students who sat around her. He was shocked to learn they didn't even know her name.

The dean of women finally told him: Liani had committed suicide.

That experience sent him on a study of how to learn and teach love. He developed a course called the Love Class. "My premise," he told the students, "is that love is learned. Our 'teachers' are the loving people we encounter.... But what would my existence have been like had I never known Liani? Would I still be stammering out subject matter at students, year after year, with little concern about the vulnerable human beings behind the masks?"

One of the assignments for the Love Class was to share something of themselves "without expectation of reward." Many volunteered to work on suicide hot lines, hoping to find the Lianis before it was too late.[10]

Provide Some Hugs

Because of the problem of abuse in our society today, adults can be afraid to hug kids. That's a crime in itself. Kids dearly need touch. The right kind. The right way. At the right time.

Dr. Ross Campbell explains many varieties of ways in which the touching need can be fulfilled for children. A nudge on the shoulder. A gentle poke in the ribs. Tousled hair. A slight hand pressure on the arm. An arm around the shoulder. A slap on the knee. A pat on the back. A playful wrestle or boxing. Bearhugs. A "give-me-five."[11]

In addition, loving eye contact with a child assigns

them worth, feeds them emotionally. Undivided attention also can answer the affirmative to that most important question a child constantly asks, if not in words, by behavior, "DO YOU LOVE ME?" The need for physical contact at every age never ceases, even though the type of physical contact can change.[12]

Every child requires an enormous store of holy hugs.

Do Your Part to Inspire:
- self-confidence (with your praise)
- a sense of adventure (with your crazy stories and ideas)
- respect (by getting close enough so they can discover you can be liked)
- courage (by telling them how you made it through problems)
- love (by giving and showing it)
- hope (by letting them know their present situation is not all there is to life)
- faith (by giving them someone to believe in, someone to care deeply about)

These four things are essential to making friends with a child, especially if he or she isn't your own:

1. *Patience.* You must be patient with their changing moods, patient with their need to have things repeated over and over, and patient with their lack of appreciation for all you do. As Mark Twain in *Adventures of Huckleberry Finn* writes:

The Widow Douglas, she took me for her son, and allowed she would sivilize me; but it was rough living in the house all the time, considering how dismal regular and decent the widow was in all her ways; and so when I couldn't stand it no longer, I lit out. I got into my old rags, and my sugar-hogshead again, and was free and satisfied. But Tom Sawyer, he hunted me up and said he was going to start a band of robbers, and I might join if I would go back to the widow and be respectable. So I went back.[13]

2. *Kindly interest*. Kids can tell when they're being tolerated or used. They respond to genuine affection and wholehearted attention. Look at them, eyeball to eyeball, and really listen to what they're trying to say.

Mrs. Macready was not fond of children, and did not like to be interrupted when she was telling visitors all the things she knew. She had said to Susan and Peter almost on the first morning (along with a good many other instructions) "And please remember you're to keep out of the way whenever I'm taking a party over the house."
"Just as if any of us would *want* to waste half the morning trailing round with a crowd of strange grown-ups!" said Edmund, and the other three thought the same. That was how the adventures began for the second time.[14]

3. *Fairness*. Children have an innate sense of justice—what's right and wrong, who's getting a fair shake, especially if it isn't them. Don't play favorites.

Said Toad, "This is my sad time of day. It is the time when I wait for the mail to come. It always makes me very unhappy."
"Why is that?" asked Frog.
"Because I never get any mail," said Toad.
"Not ever?" said Frog.

117

"No, never," said Toad. "No one has ever sent me a letter. Every day my mailbox is empty. That is why waiting for the mail is a sad time for me."

Frog and Toad sat on the porch, feeling sad together.[15]

4. *Remembering Back to What It's Like.* A child has his or her own way of thinking, of seeing the world. Read some good children's books to help your memory. See adults again from their point of view.

"Grown-ups never understand anything for themselves, and it is tiresome for children to be always and forever explaining things to them."[16]

"I'd love to call you Aunt Marilla," said Anne wistfully. "I've never had an aunt or any relation at all—not even a grandmother. It would make me feel as if I really belonged to you. Can't I call you Aunt Marilla?"

"No. I'm not your aunt and I don't believe in calling people names that don't belong to them."

"But we could imagine you were my aunt."

"I couldn't," said Marilla grimly.

"Do you never imagine things different from what they really are?" asked Anne wide-eyed.

"No."

"Oh!" Anne drew a long breath. "Oh, Miss—Marilla, how much you miss!"[17]

You can function without a child—a youth that you watch mature, unfold, and even thrive, right before your eyes; but you won't experience the full measure of what life has to offer.

It's a shameful waste of your love—love that could keep on giving, longer than your lifetime.

TIME TO CONSIDER

1. Who are the children in your life? Write down their names, ages, and their relationship to you.

2. Which of these children especially needs your attention and commitment right now? Why?

3. How long has it been since you read to (or played with) a child? List the games, activities, and books you've found most effective and enjoyable for children.

4. What did Jesus think about children?
   a. Matthew 18:1-6
   b. Matthew 19:13-15
Also check out:
   Mark 10:13-16
   Luke 9:46-48
   Luke 18:15-17

5. List at least six actions that would help a child feel loved, wanted, and cared about.
   a.   d.
   b.   e.
   c.   f.

10
···
A Friend for Life and Eternity

A tall woman suited in teal green Pendleton stood poised at the main desk. "How do I get to the penthouse?"

"You must take the private elevator, one rider at a time," replied the trim, gray-haired male attendant.

The woman drummed her long nails on the counter and peered nervously around the packed lobby. She noticed an intense man in jogging sweats waving an arm in her direction.

She tried to ignore him, but he swooped down on her. "Are you wanting to get into the penthouse to see the man, too?" he blurted out.

"Why, yes. But, you see, I received a special invitation," she began in a voice that clearly inferred she was sure he did not.

"Oh, sure. Well, I call tell you one thing. I'm not

waiting around in this jam for any one-rider elevator. There's got to be some stairs." He craned his neck around while he sprinted in place.

"I'm sorry. I haven't seen any . . ."

"Never mind. I'll ask someone. Hey, Peterson," he yelled to the man behind the desk, "where's the stairs?"

"Young man, the stairway is at the north end of the entry. However, I'm afraid it won't do you any good . . ."

The jogger didn't stick around to hear the rest. He grabbed a couple of weathered tan leather suitcases, rudely pushed aside a shawled, white-haired lady, and smacked into a potted palm tree. Eventually he wound his way to what looked like the base of a stairwell.

The Pendleton-clad woman began easing her way through the throng, until Mr. Peterson called out, "Wouldn't take the stairs if I were you, ma'am."

The woman's pride swelled like a sleeping cobra aroused from his nap.

Mr. Peterson continued. "Oh, nothing personal. The stairs don't go all the way to the penthouse. They stop on the 113th floor. The penthouse is on the 114th. That elevator's the only way up, and it opens only at the penthouse and down here in the lobby."[1]

No doubt about it. Some people are difficult to get to know. They're remote, exclusive, unavailable. They don't run in your circles. They're as distant from you as a man in a penthouse on the 114th floor.

That's what some people think about God.

Who can know him?

Where can he be found?

Does he even exist?

If he does, what's he like?

Would he be interested in a personal relationship with the likes of me?

Or you?

Wouldn't such a being, if he did reside anywhere in our universe, want to leave some clues or messages on the one inhabited planet? Wouldn't he want to make some kind of contact with other living creatures? Perhaps he would send light signals? Or roar from the heavens? Or write a book?

The Bible looms high above all the literature of the world as an outstanding work. More than forty authors. Sixty-six different "books." At least sixteen hundred years to complete. An incredible unity tying it together from beginning to end.

This tome tells people of whatever race or culture or century how to live.

This book challenges the deepest held beliefs of the human heart.

This book of books gives us an understanding of God: who he is, what he has done, and how to know him on a personal, individual basis.

WHO IS THE GOD OF THE BIBLE?

Our Creator

(Read Genesis 1, 2.)

The one who made us. The one who got this entire celestial drama rolling. Humans and orangutans. Mount Everest and the Grand Canyon. Oceans, seas, and continental drifts. All were his idea. He created them all. Just by thinking about it. Just by saying the words.

"Let there be light!" And there was light. And it was very good light.

Just for Adam's benefit. For Eve's pleasure. To give them freedom to explore and discover. At the time, they had the personal privilege of a close friendship with the Lord of it all. No 114th floor penthouse. He strolled in the garden with Adam and Eve.

Friends Forever

A Fair Judge

(Read Genesis 3; 4:1-6; Psalm 75:6-8; 2 Peter 3:7.)

Some glitches broke this idyllic picture. Adam and Eve messed up the perfect family setting, broke the original mold, slashed the pastoral painting. All was peace, prosperity, and perfection in the fertile garden. They just couldn't stand it. They couldn't be satisfied with perfection. Was it boredom? Mere curiosity? Plain ignorance? They had to test things out, try their wings, make their own decisions, risk rejection.

God's been meting out various sentences ever since. With restraint. With patience. Like a loving father who must settle the inevitable quarrels. This Father has an all-seeing eye on a phenomenal destination, an all-encompassing end.

His individual friendships include rulers and headline makers: kings and presidents and unsung heroes. They include prisoners and down-and-outers. They include average people like you and me. History's going someplace. It will all make sense some day. His justice will finally be the rule again.

A Father Seeking His Children

"Hear, O heavens! Listen, O earth! For the Lord has spoken: 'I reared children and brought them up, but they have rebelled against me' " (Isa. 1:2).

The Lord God, creator and judge, knows the pains of disappointed parents and broken relationships. His children, his own creation, disobey, rebel, run away, and refuse his offer of love. Yet he continues to use every possible means to draw them back to himself.

God is the perfect lifetime friend. Everything you ever craved for in a human relationship, and found lacking, can be found in him.

• He's alert to your every need (2 Chron. 16:9; Ps.

33:13-15; 139; Matt. 7:11).

• He knows how to sympathize (1 John 3:19, 20).

• He's patient with you (2 Pet. 3:9).

• He can protect you (Gen. 28:15; Ex. 9:26; Ps. 91).

• He can be like a husband (Isa. 54:4, 5).

• He can be like a father (Isa. 64:8; Matt. 6:9; Gal. 4:4-6).

• He forgives easily (1 John 1:9; 1 John 2:1).

• He keeps his promises (Rom. 4:18-21; Titus 1:2; Heb. 10:23).

• He has no faults (Deut. 32:4; 2 Sam. 22:31).

• He's a wise counselor (2 Sam. 22:29, 30; Ps. 32:8; Prov. 3:5, 6).

• He prods you to be and do your best (Heb. 12:5-13).

• His deep love for you gives you the confidence to risk loving others (John 3:16; Rom. 5:6-8; Eph. 2:4; 1 John 4:7-10).

Forming a relationship with us that is far deeper than anything we can possibly know among people is the way God has of challenging and inspiring us to yearn for this same divine depth in all of our human friendships. Were it not for the profound and intuitive knowledge of the Lord in our hearts, we could not know what depth of relationship is and would never miss or long for it on the human level. And so the very distance we feel from the person we love most dearly may be, paradoxically, a measure of the overwhelming closeness of God.[2]

When you enter into a relationship with God, it's permanent. He won't desert you—even in old age. In fact, this life's interaction is only the beginning. There's another life to come. With no end. Every relationship in the place the Bible calls "heaven" enters a whole new realm. Of harmony. Of intimacy. Of a kind we only taste in an occasional rare blissful moment here on earth.

When you're a friend of God's, he helps you with all your relationships. With your family. With your friends. With the estrangements. Even with your enemies.[3]

But these relationships don't fall into line immediately or even automatically. They're a process, happening as he lovingly leads you on your adventures together.

Meanwhile, he shares with you some of the mysteries of life that have always eluded you. A whole world of ideas and understanding brings a creative slant to your circumstances. You find a meaning for your existence, a purpose for your abilities. Life may not get rosier, but it will always be richer. He provides well for his friends, in this life and the next.[4]

The best part of all is that he already knows *you* well. He knows you better than you know yourself. He has been close by throughout the years, though you may never have recognized his presence or, at times, his intervention. Centuries ago, he accomplished an incredible act of sacrifice on your behalf.[5]

Where do you begin? How do you approach this supreme, supernatural being? Especially if you still have doubts and plenty of questions?

GETTING TO KNOW HIM

There are, first of all, only certain types of folks who dare approach God. You have to fall into at least one of these categories to get his attention.
- those with trusting hearts, like children
- sincere seekers
- the persistent
- the humble

• the meek
• those with the ability to show respect, honor, reverence, and obedience to a superior
• those who desperately need to be shown mercy
• the poor
• those who care about the oppressed
• cheerful givers
• those who call out to him
• those who take a step his way[6]

Irina Ratushinskaya, a human-rights activist from Russia, was a sincere seeker. She has written of her experiences growing up in a repressive society that actively denies the existence of God.

> I decided to figure out who God is. I realized that when adults tell you there are no gremlins, they tell you once, and that's it. But my teachers told us over and over again that there was no God. Because they felt they had to *keep* telling us, I knew he must exist. ... There was no Bible in our house. ... But I did like to read. ... I read the great Russian classic writers —Pushkin, Dostoevsky. ... I found that if I put together all the pieces where those writers mentioned God, I could see that God is someone who wants us to love him, love others—and especially important to me, that God is someone who always cares. ... I was 23 when I was able to read the Bible for the first time ... and realized, *I am a Christian.*[7]

And then, the second step: you've got to find the private, single-rider elevator; that is, his Son Jesus. He's still on the 114th floor of the penthouse, for all you know. Distant. Aloof. A sovereign majesty who requires a gold embossed invitation. Until you reach out to Jesus. Then, suddenly, you open the door and find he's been close all the time. Waiting for you with outstretched arms.

He made it that way on purpose. Because there's a tremendous barrier to overcome: your rebellion. He's got to test your true intent. To see if you really want to know him or just want a way out of your problems. To see if you recognize that you can't find the way by yourself, that you need help. He provided an elevator; that is, a gate, a sort of entrance. A way. One way. And there's no back door.

Jesus is the only person who ever existed that can reconcile you to God. His Father can be your Father.

Jesus. Study his life. Study his death. Study his resurrection. "If you have seen me, you have seen the Father," Jesus said. "I am in the Father, and . . . the Father is in me."[8]

He helps you find the way. He helps you know the truth. He helps you know what life's all about. He is the only one who can bring you to God. Every other person or system or philosophy that claims otherwise is taking you up the stairs to the penthouse. It's a long hike to the 113th floor. For nothing.

Charles Colson, former White House hatchet man for President Nixon, was a seeker. In the midst of the Watergate mess, he sought out an old friend of his, Tom Phillips.

A prickly feeling ran down my spine. Maybe what I had gone through in the past several months wasn't so unusual after all—except I had not sought spiritual answers. I had not even been aware that finding a personal relationship with God was possible. I pressed him [Tom] to explain the apparent contradiction between the emptiness inside while seeming to enjoy the affluent life.

"It may be hard to understand," Tom chuckled. "But I didn't seem to have anything that mattered. It

128

was all on the surface. All the material things in life are meaningless if a man hasn't discovered what's underneath them."

Tom then explained about a visit he made to a Billy Graham crusade in Madison Square Garden.

"That's what you mean by accepting Christ—you just ask?" I was more puzzled than ever.

"That's it, as simple as that," Tom replied.[9]

People. They are your main project while you stroll through this world. Whatever you're doing, wherever you live, people count. Giving. Committing. Caring. Even earning. That all involves people. It's a life's work.

Concentrating on others can be difficult, if not impossible, if . . .

You don't see the point in it all. In that case, you might as well keep on living for yourself.

You haven't found peace with yourself. You don't have a balanced view of who you are. And who you are not.

You're stuck on all your pet peeves. You might as well sit in your soundproof TV room and shut the world out.

You're stranded on a lonely, deserted island because of your anger.

Perhaps you've never learned how to make up when the relationship's broken down.

Or you're still fighting with Mom or Dad.

Or the relationship with your husband is no better.

And so many needy kids are all around. Where to begin?

It can be overwhelming. People relationships get so confusing sometimes. With no easy formula. At least you can settle on your goal. You can determine what's of utmost importance to you. Then, you'll know where to head.

The Bible explains the prime pursuit of anyone who's serious about the true purpose of this life and how to prepare for the life to come.

It's simple. It's clear. It's life changing.

" 'Love the Lord your God with all your heart and with all your soul and with all your mind.' This is the first and greatest commandment. And the second is like it: 'Love your neighbor as yourself. All the Law and Prophets hang on these two commandments' " (Matt. 22:37-40).

Learn to love God.

Learn to love your neighbor.

Learn to love (accept, be comfortable with, be at peace with, have a balanced view of) yourself.

That's it.

That's all.

That's enough to last a lifetime.

TIME TO CONSIDER

1. Write a description of the first time you became aware of God's presence in your life.

2. Describe your relationship with God right now.

3. List five things you know about Jesus.
   a.
   b.
   c.
   d.
   e.

4. What does Jesus mean to you?

5. Prepare a weekly schedule of Bible reading that is realistic, that fits your lifestyle, and that you could con-

tinue for a year. Find a friend to keep you accountable to this goal, to whom you can go with questions and sharing of discoveries.

6. Think about the following words: "What good will it be for a man if he gains the whole world, yet forfeits his soul?" (Matt. 16:26). What does this have to say about your priorities? About your relationships?

Source Notes

Chapter 1

1. Bill Moyers, *A World of Ideas* (New York: Doubleday, 1989), p. vii.

2. Clyde M. Narramore, *How to Succeed in Family Living* (Glendale, CA: Regal Books, 1968), p. 2.

3. William W. Sweet, *The Story of Religion in America* (Grand Rapids, MI: Baker Book House, 1973), p. 128.

4. Clyde E. Fant, Jr., and William M. Pinson, Jr., *20 Centuries of Great Preaching* (Waco, TX: Word Books, 1971), pp. 49, 50.

5. *Today in the Word* (Chicago: Moody Bible Institute, April 1989), p. 42. Devotional pamphlet.

6. Dee Brestin, "Hang on to Your Friends . . . Your Health Could Depend on It," *Today's Christian Woman*, March/April 1990, p. 30.

7. Daniel Goleman, "Resilient Kids Can Beat Odds," *New York Times News Service* in *Ventura County Star Free Press,* October 19, 1987, p. B1.

8. Moyers, p. viii.

9. George Eliot, [Marian Evans Cross], "Friendship," *The Speaker's Sourcebook* (Grand Rapids, MI: Zondervan Publishing House, 1960), p. 107.

10. Barbara Evans, *Joy! Correspondence with Pat Boone* (Carol Stream: IL: Creation House, 1973).

11. Gloria H. Hawley, *How to Teach the Mentally Retarded* (Wheaton, IL: Victor Books, 1978).

12. David Wilkerson with John and Elizabeth Sherrill, *The Cross and the Switchblade* (Pyramid Publications, 1963).

13. Elisabeth Elliot, "Amy Carmichael of India," from *Bright Legacy,* ed. Ann Spangler (Ann Arbor, MI: Servant Publications, 1983).

14. John Bartlett, *Familiar Quotations* (Boston: Little, Brown and Company, 1855). p. 354:4, from a letter Samuel Johnson wrote to Lord Chesterfield in 1755.

Chapter 2

1. Edwin Markham, "Outwitted," *The Book of Poetry,* vol. 1 (New York: Wm. H. Wise & Co., 1928), p. 265.

2. Ellen Hawkes, "She's My Best Friend," *Parade* in *The Lewiston Morning Tribune,* December 3, 1989, pp. 4, 5.

3. L.M. Montgomery, *Anne of Green Gables* (New York: Bantam Books, 1908), p. 57.

4. Stephen Bly and Janet Bly, *Be Your Mate's Best Friend* (Chicago: Moody Press, 1989), pp. 120, 121.

5. Kitty Muggeridge, "Where Charity and Love Begin," *Worldwide Challenge,* June 1988, p. 77.

Chapter 3

1. Janet Chester Bly, "Entry," *Insight* and *Touch*, February 1980, and *Alive! for Young Teens,* July 1988.

2. Dr. James Dobson, "Hide or Seek," *Sunday Digest,* June/July/August 1979, sect. 13, p. 5.

3. Allan Bloom, *The Closing of the American Mind* (New York: Simon & Schuster, Inc., 1987), p. 119.

4. Ted Engstrom with Robert C. Larson, "Cranberries and Shoeshines," *Servant,* March/April 1989, p. 3.

5. C.S. Lewis, "The Requirements of Love," Christian Classics, Penelope J. Stokes, *Sunday Digest,* November 1987, sect. 13, p. 8.

6. "Hide or Seek," pp. 5, 6.

Chapter 4

1. Henry Drummond, *The Greatest Thing in the World* (Mount Vernon, NY: The Peter Pauper Press), p. 29.

2. Charles Erdman, *The First Epistle of Paul to the Corinthians* (Philadelphia: The Westminster Press, 1928), p. 119.

3. Robert H. Schuller, *Tough Times Never Last, But Tough People Do!* (Nashville: Thomas Nelson Publishers, 1983), p. 71.

4. Charles Panati, *Extraordinary Origins of Everyday Things* (New York: Harper & Row Publishers, 1987), p. 388.

5. John Claypool, "A Pattern for Coping," *The Light Within You* (Waco, TX: Word Books, 1983), p. 116.

Chapter 5

1. Jay E. Adams, *You Can Defeat Anger* (Grand Rapids, MI: Baker Book House, 1975), p. 9.

2. John Claypool, "A Pattern for Coping," *The Light Within You* (Waco, TX: Word Books, 1983), p. 119.

3. Mary Long, "Why We Love Our Friends to Fail," *Family Weekly* in *Ventura County Star Free Press,* August 8, 1982, p. 12.

4. Tim LaHaye and Bev LaHaye, *Spirit Controlled Family Living* (Old Tappan, NJ: Fleming H. Revell Company, 1978), p. 55.

Chapter 6

1. For further study on this subject, read: Genesis 3; Matthew 13:19, 38; Romans 8:19-25; 2 Corinthians 4:4; 1 Thessalonians 3:5, 6; 1 Peter 5:8, 9; Revelation 12:7-9.

2. Eugene Kennedy, *On Being a Friend* (New York: Epiphany/Ballantine Books, 1989), cover copy

3. For further study on these two subjects, read: Romans 7:15-25; Ephesians 2:1-5; 6:10-18; James 3:2-12; 4:1, 2.

4. Norman B. Rohrer and S. Philip Sutherland, *Why Am I Shy?* (Minneapolis: Augsburg Publishing House, 1978).

5. Chuck Christenson and Winnie Christenson, "Advice," *Moody Monthly,* November 1989, p. 32.

Chapter 7

1. Janet Chester Bly, "The Road Most Traveled," copyright 1989.

2. Gary Smalley and John Trent, Ph.D., *Love Is a Decision* (Phoenix: Today's Family, 1989), p. 81.

3. See 1 Timothy 5:1-4.

4. Ross Snyder, *On Becoming Human* (Nashville: Abingdon Press, 1967), p. 94.

5. Lawrence Kutner, "Childhood Friendships," *The New*

York Times in *The Lewiston Tribune,* December 1988, p. 2A.

6. Ross Snyder, pp. 100, 101.

7. Ellen Goodman, "When an Aging Aunt Hands You the Bird," *The Boston Globe* in *The Lewiston Tribune,* November 23, 1989, p. 1F.

8. Stephen Bly and Janet Bly, "When She's Not So Nice, Guidelines to Loving Mom," *Christian Life Magazine,* May 1987, p. 33.

9. "When an Aging Aunt Hands You the Bird," p. 1F.

Chapter 8

1. Janet C. Bly, "I Do . . . You Don't!," *Sunday Digest,* November 2, 1986, p. 2.

2. Richard and Mary Strauss, "Working Through Marital Conflict," *Focus on the Family,* March 1989, p. 3.

3. Harville Hendrix, Ph.D., "That Loving Feeling," *The Family Circle,* July 25, 1989, p. 62.

4. Mike Mason, *The Mystery of Marriage* (Portland: Multnomah Press, 1985), p. 149.

5. Gary Chapman, *Toward a Growing Marriage* (Chicago: Moody Press, 1979), p. 107.

6. Dr. Charles Sell, *Achieving the Impossible: Intimate Marriage* (New York: Epiphany/Ballantine Books, 1986), cover copy.

7. Joseph M. Stowell, "Making Marriage Stick," Front Lines, *Moody Monthly,* February 1989, p. 4.

8. Abraham Maslow, *Motivation and Personality* (New York: Harper, 1954), p. 236.

9. "That Loving Feeling," p. 62.

10. *Dear Abby, The Lewiston Tribune,* February 20, 1989, p. 7B.

Chapter 9

1. See Matthew 18:2-6; Mark 9:36, 37; 10:15; Luke 9:46-48.

2. Jacob Abbott, from *The New Dictionary of Thoughts* (New York: Standard Book Company, 1955), p. 517.

3. Kate Douglas Wiggin, from *The New Dictionary of Thoughts* p. 75.

4. Dr. Julie A. Gorman, "The World of Children," *Theology, News and Notes,* March 1987, Fuller Theological Seminary, p. 3.

5. "The World of Children," p. 4.

6. George Eliot, [Marian Evans Cross], from *The New Dictionary of Thoughts* p. 75.

7. Aristotle, from *The Speaker's Sourcebook* com. Eleanor Doan (Grand Rapids: Zondervan Publishing House, 1960), p. 49.

8. Corrie ten Boom with C.C. Carlson, *In My Father's House* (Old Tappan, NJ: Fleming H. Revell Company, 1976), pp. 139, 140.

9. Robert Burns, "On the Late Captain Grose's Peregrinations Thro' Scotland," from *Familiar Quotations* by John Bartlett (Boston: Little, Brown and Company, 1855), p. 410.

10. Leo Buscaglia, "The Girl in the Fifth Row," *Reader's Digest,* September 1984, pp. 33-40.

11. Dr. Ross Campbell, "How to Really Love Your Child," *Worldwide Challenge,* May/June 1990, p. 30.

12. Ibid., pp. 27, 28.

13. Mark Twain, *Adventures of Huckleberry Finn* (Boston: Houghton Mifflin Company, 1958), p. 3.

14. C.S. Lewis, *The Lion, the Witch, and the Wardrobe,* from *The Chronicles of Narnia* (New York: Religious Book Club, 1973), p. 41.

15. Arnold Lobel, *Frog and Toad Are Friends* (New York: Harper & Row, 1970), pp. 54, 55.

16. Antoine de Saint-Exupery, *The Little Prince,* from *Familiar Quotations,* p. 849.

17. L.M. Montgomery, *Anne of Green Gables* (New York: Bantam Books, 1908), pp. 54, 55.

Chapter 10

1. Stephen A. Bly, adapted from the parable, "There's No Back Door," *Young Ambassador,* June 1977, pp. 26, 27.

2. Mike Mason, *The Mystery of Marriage* (Portland: Multnomah Press, 1985), p. 33.

3. See Psalm 127:1; Proverbs 16:7; Isaiah 46:4; 49: 25; John 14:2; 2 Corinthians 5:18, 19.

4. See Proverbs 9:10; Hosea 13:4; Matthew 6:33; John 14:19; 17:3; Romans 6:23; 2 Timothy 4:8.

5. See Genesis 28:16; Jeremiah 1:5; 23:23, 24; Psalm 139:13-16; Acts 17:27; Romans 5:6-8.

6. See Exodus 33:11; 1 Samuel 7:3; Ezra 8:22; Psalm 10:17; 145:18; 147:11; Isaiah 29:19; Matthew 5:5; Luke 10:21; John 4:23; 2 Corinthians 9:7; James 4:8; Revelation 3:5.

7. Ellen Santilli Vaughn, "In Solitary Cells on Winter Nights," *Christianity Today,* December 15, 1989. p. 28.

8. See John 14:6-11.

9. Charles Colson, *Born Again* (published by Chosen Books, distributed by Old Tappan, NJ: Fleming H. Revell Company, 1976), pp. 109, 110.

Support Group Leader's Guide

Issue-oriented, problem-wrestling, life-confronting—Aglow Publications' Heart Issue books are appropriate for adult Sunday school classes, individual study, and especially for support groups. Here are guidelines to encourage and facilitate support groups.

SUPPORT GROUP GUIDELINES

The small group setting offers individuals the opportunity to commit themselves to personal growth through mutual caring and support. This is especially true of Christian support groups, where from five to twelve individuals meet on a regular basis with a mature leader to share their personal experiences and struggles over a specific "heart issue." In such a group, individuals develop trust and accountability with each other and the Lord.

Because a support group's purpose differs from a Bible study or prayer group, it needs its own format and guidelines.

Let's look at the ingredients of a support group:
- Purpose
- Leadership
- Group Leadership Skills
- Meeting Format
- Group Guidelines

PURPOSE

The purpose of a Heart Issue support group is to provide:

1. An *opportunity* for participants to share openly and honestly their struggles and pain over a specific issue in a non-judgmental, Christ-centered framework.

2. A *"safe place"* where participants can gain perspective on a mutual problem and begin taking responsibility for their responses to their own situations.

3. An *atmosphere* that is compassionate, understanding, and committed to challenging participants from a biblical perspective.

Support groups are not counseling groups. Participants come to be supported, not fixed or changed. Yet, as genuine love and caring are exchanged, people begin to experience God's love and acceptance. As a result, change and healing take place.

The initiators of a support group need to be clear about its specific purpose. The following questions are examples of what to consider before starting a small group.

1. What type of group will this be? A personal growth group, a self-help group, or a group structured to focus on a certain theme? Is it long-term, short-term, or ongoing?

2. Who is the group for? A particular population?

College students? Single women? Divorced people?

3. What are the goals for the group? What will members gain from it?

4. Who will lead or co-lead the group? What are his/her qualifications?

5. How many members should be in the group? Will new members be able to join the group once it is started?

6. What kind of structure or format will the group have?

7. What topics will be explored in the support group and to what degree will this be determined by the group members and to what degree by the leaders?

LEADERSHIP

Small group studies often rotate leadership among participants, but because support groups usually meet for a specific time period with a specific mutual issue, it works well to have one leader or a team of co-leaders responsible for the meetings.

Good leadership is essential for a healthy, balanced group. Qualifications include character and personality traits as well as life experience and, in some cases, professional experience.

Personal Leadership Characteristics
COURAGE

One of the most important traits of effective group leaders is courage. Courage is shown in willingness (1) to be open to self-disclosure, admitting their own mistakes and taking the same risks they expect others to take; (2) to confront another, and, in confronting, to understand that love is the goal; (3) to act on their beliefs and hunches; (4) to be emotionally touched by another and to draw on their experiences in order to identify with the other; (5) to continually examine their inner selves; (6) to be direct and honest with members; and (7) to express to the group their fears and expectations about the group process. (Leaders shouldn't use their role to protect themselves from honest and direct interaction with the rest of the group.)

WILLINGNESS TO MODEL

Through their behavior and the attitudes conveyed by it, leaders can create a climate of openness, seriousness of purpose, acceptance of others, and the desirability of taking risks. Group leaders should have had some moderate victory in their own struggles, with adequate healing having taken place. They recognize their own woundedness and see themselves as persons in process as well. Group leaders lead largely by example—by doing what they expect members to do.

PRESENCE

Group leaders need to be emotionally present with the group members. This means being touched by others' pain, struggles, and joys. Leaders can become more emotionally involved with others by paying close attention to their own reactions and by permitting these reactions to become intense. Fully experiencing emotions gives leaders the ability to be compassionate and empathetic with their members. At the same time, group leaders understand their role as facilitators. They know they're not answer people; they don't take responsibility for change in others.

GOODWILL AND CARING

A sincere interest in the welfare of the others is essential in group leaders. Caring involves respecting, trusting, and valuing people. Not every member is easy to care for, but leaders should at least want to care. It is vital that leaders become aware of the kinds of people they care for easily and the kinds they find it difficult to care for. They can gain this awareness by openly exploring their reactions to members. Genuine caring must be demonstrated; merely saying so is not enough.

Some ways to express a caring attitude are: (1) inviting a person to participate but allowing that person to decide how far to go; (2) giving warmth, concern, and support when, and only when, it is genuinely felt; (3) gently confronting the person when there are obvious discrepancies between a person's words and her behavior; and (4) encouraging people to be what they could be without their masks and shields. This kind of caring requires a commitment to love and a sensitivity to the Holy Spirit.

OPENNESS

To be effective, group leaders must be open with themselves, open to others in groups, open to new experiences, and open to life-styles and values that differ from their own. Openness is an attitude. It doesn't mean that leaders reveal every aspect of their personal lives; it means that they reveal enough of themselves to give the participants a sense of person.

Leader openness tends to foster a spirit of openness within the group; it permits members to become more open about their feelings and beliefs; and it lends a certain fluidity to the group process. Self-revelation should not be manipulated as a technique. However, self-evaluation is best done spontaneously, when appropriate.

NONDEFENSIVENESS

Dealing frankly with criticism is related closely to openness. If group leaders are easily threatened, insecure in their work of leading, overly sensitive to negative feedback, and depend highly on group approval, they will probably encounter major problems in trying to carry out their leadership role. Members sometimes accuse leaders of not caring enough, of being selective in their caring, of structuring the sessions too much, of not providing enough direction, of being too harsh. Some criticism may be fair, some unfair. The crucial thing for leaders is to non-defensively explore with their groups the feelings that are legitimately produced by the leaders and those that represent what is upsetting the member.

STRONG SENSE OF SELF

A strong sense of self (or personal power) is an important quality of leaders. This doesn't mean that leaders would manipulate or dominate; it means that leaders are confident of who they are and what they are about. Groups "catch" this and feel the leaders know what they are doing. Leaders who have a strong sense of self recognize their weaknesses and don't expend energy concealing them from others. Their vulnerability becomes their strength as leaders. Such leaders can accept credit where it's due and, at the same time, encourage members to accept credit for their own growth.

STAMINA

Group leading can be taxing and draining as well as exciting and energizing. Leaders need physical and emotional stamina and the ability to withstand pressure in order to remain vitalized until the group sessions end. If leaders give in to fatigue when the group bogs down, becomes resistive, or when members drop out, the effectiveness of the whole group could suffer. Leaders must be aware of their own energy level, have outside sources of spiritual and emotional nourishment, and have realistic expectations for the group's progress.

SENSE OF HUMOR

The leaders who enjoy humor and can incorporate it appropriately into the group will bring a valuable asset to the meetings. Sometimes humor surfaces as an escape from healthy confrontations and sensitive leaders need to identify and help the group avoid this diversion. But because we often take ourselves and our problems too seriously, we need the release of humor to bring balance and perspective. This is particularly true after sustained periods of dealing seriously with intensive problems.

CREATIVITY

The capacity to be spontaneously creative, to approach each group session with fresh ideas is a most important characteristic for group leaders. Leaders who are good at discovering new ways of approaching a group and who are willing to suspend the use of established techniques are unlikely to grow stale. Working with interesting co-leaders is another way for leaders to acquire fresh ideas.

GROUP LEADERSHIP SKILLS

Although personality characteristics of the group leader are extremely significant, by themselves they do not ensure a healthy group. Leadership skills are also essential. The following traits need to be expressed in a sensitive and timely way:

ACTIVE LISTENING

Leaders need to absorb content, note gestures, observe subtle changes in voice or expression, and sense underlying messages. For example, a woman may be talking about her warm and loving feelings toward her husband, yet her body may be rigid and her fists clenched.

EMPATHY

This requires sensing the subjective world of the participant. Group leaders, in addition to being caring and open, must learn to grasp another's experience and at the same time maintain their separateness.

RESPECT AND POSITIVE REGARD

In giving support, leaders need to draw on the positive assets of the members. Where differences occur, there needs to be open and honest appreciation and toleration.

147

WARMTH

Smiling has been shown to be especially important in the communication of warmth. Other nonverbal means are: voice tone, posture, body language, and facial expression.

GENUINENESS

Leaders need to be real, to be themselves in relating with others, to be authentic and spontaneous.

MEETING FORMAT

The format of meetings will differ vastly from group to group, but the following are generally accepted as working well with support groups.

MEETING PLACE

This should be a comfortable, warm atmosphere. Participants need to feel welcome and that they've come to a "safe place" where they won't be overheard or easily distracted. Some groups will want to provide baby-sitting.

OPENING

Welcome participants. The leader should introduce herself and the members should also introduce themselves. It is wise to go over the "ground rules" at every meeting and especially at first or when there are newcomers. Some of these would include:

1. Respect others' sharing by keeping what is said in the group confidential.

2. Never belittle the beliefs or expressions of another.

3. Respect the time schedule. Try to arrive on time and be prompt in leaving.

4. Feel free to contact the leader at another time if you have questions or need additional help.

Many meetings open with a brief time of prayer and worship and conclude with prayer. It often helps to ask for informal prayer requests and brief sharing so that the group begins in a spirit of openness.

MEETING

Leaders can initiate the meeting by focusing on a particular issue (or chapter if the group is studying a book). It is wise to define the focus of the specific meeting so that the group can stay on track for the entire session. (See Group Guidelines below.)

CLOSING

Strive for promptness without being abrupt. Give opportunity for those who need additional help to make an appointment with the leader. Be alert to those needing special affirmation or encouragement as they leave.

GROUP GUIDELINES

Because this is a support group, not an advice group, the leader will need to establish the atmosphere and show by her style how to relate lovingly and helpfully within the group. Participants need to know the guidelines for being a member of the group. It is a wise practice to repeat these guidelines at each meeting and especially when newcomers attend. The following guidelines have proven to be helpful to share with support groups:

1. You have come to give and receive support. No "fixing." We are to listen, support, and be supported by one another—not give advice.

2. Let other members talk. Please let them finish without interruption.

3. Try to step over any fear of sharing in the group. Yet do not monopolize the group's time.

4. Be interested in what someone else is sharing. Listen with your heart. Never converse privately with someone else while another member is addressing the group.

5. Be committed to expressing your feelings from the

heart. Encourage others to do the same. It's all right to feel angry, to laugh, or to cry.

6. Help others own their feelings and take responsibility for change in their lives. Don't jump in with an easy answer or a story on how you conquered their problem. Relate to where they are.

7. Avoid accusing or blaming. Speak in the "I" mode about how something or someone made *you* feel. Example: "I felt angry when. . . ."

8. Avoid ill-timed humor to lighten emotionally charged times. Let participants work through their sharing even if it is hard.

9. Keep names and sharing of other group members confidential.

10. Because we are all in various stages of growth, please give newcomers permission to be new and old-timers permission to be further along in their growth. This is a "safe place" for all to grow and share their lives.

For correspondence or speaking
engagements, contact:

Janet Chester Bly
Box 157
Winchester,Idaho 83555